CARTOONING

WASHINGTON

CARTOONING

WASHINGTON

One Hundred Years of Cartoon Art
in the Evergreen State

Edited by Maury Forman and Rick Marschall

Text by Glen Baron

MELIOR PUBLICATIONS

Spokane, Washington

Cartoon compilation copyright © 1989 by Cartoon, Inc. Text material
copyright © 1989 by Glen Baron. All rights reserved. No part of this book
may be reproduced, stored in a retrieval system, or transmitted in any
form, or by any means electronic, mechanical, photocopying, or
otherwise, without the prior written permission of Melior Publications.
Copyrighted cartoons are used by permission of the artist and/or
newspaper. Others are in the public domain.
Published by Melior Publications, P.O. Box 1905, Spokane, Washington
99210-1905, (509) 455-9617. Printed in the United States of America.
ISBN 0-9616441-8-4

93 92 91 90 89 5 4 3 2 1

Library of Congress Cataloging-in-Publication Data
Cartooning Washington : one hundred years of cartoon art in
 the Evergreen State / edited by Maury B. Forman and Richard E.
 Marschall; text by Glen Baron.
      p. cm.
   ISBN 0-9616441-7-6 : $24.95. — ISBN 0-9616441-8-4 (pbk.): $13.95
   1. Washington (State)—Politics and government—1889– 1950—
Caricatures and cartoons. 2.Washington (State)—Politics and
government—1951– —Caricatures and cartoons. 3. American wit and
 humor, Pictorial. I. Forman, Marury B., 1950– . II. Marschall,
 Richard. III. Baron, Glen, 1950– .
 F891.C34 1989
 979.7'04'0207—dc20   89-39130
                                         CIP

Table of Contents

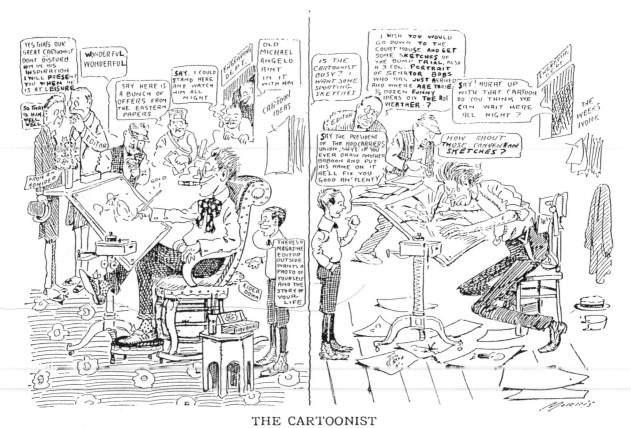

THE CARTOONIST

The popular conception   The reality

Acknowledgements

Cartoon, Inc. is a Washington corporation devoted to the preservation, display, and celebration of America's cartooning heritage. Its founders are Rick Marschall, comics historian and critic, and Maury Forman, collector and administrator, and they were pleasantly surprised when the 1989 Washington Centennial Commission asked Washington citizens to imagine new ways to contribute to the state's centennial observances.

Maury Forman conceived the idea of a museum quality exhibit that would highlight Washington's history entirely through cartoons. As this book, and the exhibit on which it is based, amply prove, Washington has had an unusually high number of cartoonists through the century. The cartoonists, through wit and keen commentary, have left a unique record from which we, today, may amuse ourselves as well as gain an insight into state history.

Countless hours spent in libraries and museums, reviewing archives and newspaper files, convinced Cartoon, Inc. that a traveling exhibit should be supplemented by a book. Hence from conception of the exhibit to completion of this book, Cartoon, Inc. would like to acknowledge the help of many who assisted.

Cartoonists: Brian Basset, *Seattle Times*; David Horsey, *Seattle Post-Intelligencer*; Frank Shiers, *T. R. Syndicate*; Al Pratt, *Seattle Times* (retired); Bob McCausland, *Seattle Post-Intelligencer* (retired); Herb Block, *Washington Post*; Paul Conrad, *Los Angeles Times*; Garry Trudeau; Walt Crowley, *Helix* (retired); Walt Partymiller; Dave McKay; Paul Fung, Jr.; and especially Shaw McCutcheon (retired) and Milt Priggee of the *Spokesman-Review* and *Spokane Chronicle*.

Historians and researchers: Corey Gregorson, Karyl Winn, and Janet Ness of the Suzzalo Library, University of Washington; Jane Walters of the *Spokesman-Review* library; staff members of the Tacoma *Morning News Tribune*; Brian Kamens, Northwest Room at the Tacoma Library; David Nicandri of the Washington State Historical Society; and Francis Hare of the Yakima Valley Museum. Special thanks to Bill Blackbeard of the San Francisco Academy of Comic Art.

Publishers and editors: Virgil Fassio and J. D. Alexander of the *Seattle Post-Intelligencer*; June Almquest of the *Seattle Times*; Barbara Krohn of *The University of Washington Daily*.

Special thanks: To our long-suffering and supportive wives, Mary Foye and Nancy Marschall; and, for financial assistance in the form of exhibit support, to the Bon Marche; and to the *Spokesman-Review* and *Spokane Chronicle*, especially Shaun Higgins, whose support for Cartoon, Inc.'s centennial project has been generous and greatly appreciated. Also meriting special thanks are Virginia Foye, Laureen Lund of the Issaquah

Centennial Commission, Wendy Terlizzi of the Pacific Medical Center, Lisa Napoli of the Henry M. Jackson Foundation, Lynn Hvalsoe, and Ernest Erke. Additional thanks to Nick Minotti, Bob Griep, Jim Clough, Bonnie Steussy, O. Leo Lahey, Rush Gook, and Ed Norton. Special thanks to Ken Becker and John Timmins for artwork touch-up. We also thank our publisher, John Shideler, and his staff members Bob Woods, Mindy Peterson, and Stéphanie Shideler, for their contributions to this project.

We would like to dedicate this book to one of Washington state's most precious natural resources, the wonderful and creative band of cartoonists who have labored over their drawing boards during the last century. They have daily bequeathed their work to us, their unseen audience, so this book is rightfully theirs.

Maury Forman

Rick Marschall

Cartoon, Inc.

I would like to thank the following people for helping me to make this book possible.

Margretta Voinot-Baron, who has always kept faith and her sense of humor; Larry Book, who told me to "go for it" and to keep swimming when the waters got dangerous; my colleagues at Kentwood High School, who guided me toward reference materials, read early drafts, and were always supportive.

Special thanks to Dr. Gerald Robison, Jean Morlan, Carolyn Rancour, Rick Comer, Barbara Boling, Susan Andrews, Mike Mullay, Al Waltner, Rick Fuerst, Joyce Hartnett, Bruce Band, Paula Eismann, Sandy Puchar, and Jack Henderson; and to students Carrie Ryan, Donna Waddell, Nicole Thrift, Meike Foster, Heather Wilson, Jason Rhodes, and Kevin Carpenter, who were always enthusiastic and eager to assist; and to Heidi Sachs for her counsel and kind words.

Thanks to all of the following people for their research assistance: Brian Limotti and Bill Southern, Washington State Department of Transportation; W. Thomas White, Curator for the James J. Hill Reference Library, Minnesota Historical Society; Ruby J. Shields, Minnesota Historical Society; Charm Arneson, Sports Information Office at Washington State University; Cindy Holt, Sports Information Office at the University of Washington; Gary Reese, Northwest Room at the Tacoma Public Library; Mark Albright, Atmospheric Sciences Department, University of Washington; Pat Hopkins and Mike Betz, Washington State Archives; Richard Keeton, Washington State POW-MIA Concerned Citizens Association, Veterans of Foreign Wars; Dan Barney, Veterans of Foreign Wars; Charlie Hodde, Washington State Grange; Glenn Hampson, Assistant to Rep. Rod Chandler; and Linda Petersen, Assistant to State Rep. Bruce Holland.

I would like to dedicate this book to the loving memory of Margretta MacFarlane Hillman who taught me the meaning of Loch Sloy.

Glen Baron

Foreword

Not long ago, I was in Washington, D.C. for what turned out to be a long and arduous hearing before the U.S. Supreme Court. After listening to a seemingly endless session of legal debate, I was definitely ready for a change of pace.

To my absolute delight, one of the locals told me about a display of historical political cartoons being shown in the Madison Wing of the Library of Congress. I spent the next several hours happily browsing through a gold mine of cartoons chronicling a host of world and national events from years gone by.

As a history buff and a devoted fan of political cartoons, I was sure it would be next to impossible to top such an experience. Only one thing could be better, I thought—a collection of political cartoons highlighting the history of our own state of Washington. So I was naturally thrilled when Dr. Maury Forman, co-founder of Cartoon, Inc., told me of plans to publish such a book during our state's one hundredth birthday celebration. What a wonderful addition to Washington's Centennial bookshelf!

Throughout American history, political cartoons have served as a mechanism to illustrate our society's triumphs and its shortcomings. More often than not, the political cartoon has been the most effective way of communicating the real meaning of those events that appeared on the front page or in the editorial section.

In the days before many citizens could read, the cartoon could deliver an instant and powerful message to the public. Thomas Nast, undoubtedly the best-known of the early political cartoonists, hammered away at the corruption of New York's "Boss" Tweed and Tammany Hall in *Harper's Weekly*. "We gotta stop them damned pictures," Tweed wailed. "I don't care so much what the papers write about me—my constituents can't read. But they can see pictures."

(It was one of "them damned pictures" that stopped Tweed. After being sentenced to jail, he escaped in 1875 and made his way to Europe. While hiding out in Spain, he was recognized from one of Nast's caricatures, arrested and returned to the United States.)

Nowadays, those who seek and hold political office haven't really lived until they've been skewered by a political cartoon in one of the weeklies or the dailies. It is a graduation of sorts; a political career cannot be considered complete until one's likeness is the subject of a withering blast from the political cartoonist. On rare occasions it is a pat on the back, but more likely it is a hard poke to the jaw or a bullet to the chest that is delivered via the cartoonist's pen.

This book is an absolute must for those who are interested in Washington state history and political science. The cartoons contained within are a barometer of sorts, often measuring the true feelings of Washingtonians at the time—and certainly in a more interesting fashion than the dry accounts written in most of our Washington state history books.

Cartooning Washington: One Hundred Years of Cartoon Art in the Evergreen State is, in short, a truly fascinating journey through the colorful political and social history of the state of Washington. I hope you enjoy the trip as much as I have.

Ralph Munro

Secretary of State

Co-Chairman

1989 Washington State Centennial Commission

Introduction

The cartoon is a unique form of expression. While it is not an art form indigenous to the United States, it certainly embodies American characteristics.

A cartoon is terse and concise; it displays aspects of virtuosity and talent; it can be pointed or philosophical, serious or humorous. If ever there were a "picture worth a thousand words," it is the cartoon. And in America it has achieved a place in the processes of decision-making and public debate. The cartoon is designed to amuse, arouse, educate, rally, and sometimes infuriate readers—and sometimes do all these things simultaneously. The American cartoonist is not just an artist but a social critic.

In retrospect we can also see that the cartoonist is a splendid reporter and historian. Cartoons are the journalistic footprints by which we can best trace the story of our recent past. Neither headlines resurrected from old microfilmed files nor researchers' charts and graphs can tell us as much about our predecessors and their times. But cartoonists are obliged to address issues of universal concern or general need; in a single image the cartoonist must sum up certain points of view, make a fresh statement, render his subject recognizable to a spectrum of readers, and mirror the fashions, styles, and attitudes of the day. Cartoons of the past speak not only about forgotten issues, but also about how people lived, what amused them, what their prejudices were, and so forth.

As such the cartoon is a remarkable social and historical document. But this importance notwithstanding, the cartoon was more honored in the past than today, at least in terms of the prominence afforded its publication. Many newspapers used to run their political cartoons on front pages, and some in color.

Benjamin Franklin was the first American to draw political cartoons. As publisher and printer, the revolutionist Franklin drafted several cartoons that persuaded colonists to rebel against England. The second American cartoonist was scarcely less famous in history: Paul Revere was a silversmith and engraver who created incendiary cartoons disguised as prints of news events.

After independence cartooning in America consisted almost entirely of political and partisan subjects. The administrations of Washington, Jefferson, and Jackson in particular were marked by a surfeit of pro and con cartoons, many of an extreme nature. By the time of Lincoln's presidency hundreds of cartoons appeared each year in magazines, newspapers, penny-prints, posters, lithographs, and broadsides. During the Civil War President Lincoln himself called cartoonist Thomas Nast the "North's best recruiting sergeant." Also it was Nast who almost single handedly defeated the corrupt Democratic machine in New York City (Tammany Hall) in 1871.

After Nast, popular national magazines like *Puck, Judge,* and *Life,* and dozens of their imitators regularly published cartoons about the events of the day. They were hugely influential. The place of the political cartoon in national discourse was recognized when the Pulitzer Prize committee in 1922 decided to judge annually the work of America's political cartoonists for their excellence and influence. Because of their importance in our national history, it is the work of political cartoonists in particular (rather than humorous or social cartoonists) that is primarily addressed in this collection.

In its one hundred years Washington state has had a generous and disproportionate share of native cartoonists to record and comment upon social and political events of interest to residents of the Evergreen State. Their work has been published throughout the state and reprinted nationally. To review a collection of the best cartoons of a hundred years is not only to share laughs and witness passionate debate, but to visit the significant issues, events, and personalities of the colorful first century of Washington statehood.

From the earliest days of statehood, and even before, there were drawings in Washington newspapers. Some were cartoons advocating certain points of view, and some were news sketches, for cartoonists had to wear several hats in the early days of their craft. State publications like the *Spokane Falls* and the *West Shore* featured cartoons. In 1892, shortly after statehood, Tacoma's weekly newspaper *New West*—a "Pictorial Journal of Current Events"—was founded by Randolf Foster Radebaugh, one of the foremost journalists and publishers of the Northwest. The paper lasted only a year, but during its life it emulated *Harper's Weekly* of New York in both its format and its fight against municipal political corruption; a campaign against extravagantly excessive light and water project costs was a major campaign. The paper proposed to publish information about the state's growing greatness in the expectation that dissemination of such news would serve to accelerate the state's growth.

The Tacoma paper's first editorial recognized the role of cartoons not only in its own publishing vision but in public policy debates in a democracy: "The object lessons of a pictorial paper have a well-recognized value in the instruction of men and women of mature minds..." (issue of November 12, 1882). Radebaugh intended his paper to be one of action, not just theory. Through his cartoons he set forth valuable ideas in connection with the

WHAT IS A MONUMENT TO BEEFSTEAK.

Tacoma: "Not much you don't! All I have left is the purse,
and have to hustle up some beefsteak—or die!"

city's improvement in the early days.

Washington's first daily political cartoonist was A. H. Lee of the *Seattle Post-Intelligencer*. Hired in 1895, his cartoons railed against Populism, a radical political movement then influential in the state. Despite Lee's salvos more than two dozen Populists were elected to the state legislature; Populist John Rogers was elected governor in 1896, and in the same year Washington was carried by the Democrat-Populist candidate for president, William Jennings Bryan.

The Democratic Party of the State of Washington
is on the inside this year.

But just a year later, Lee's attention—and Washington's —was diverted to other matters when the steamer "Portland" sailed into Seattle's Elliot Bay with news of the gold strike in the Klondike. As Seattle became the gateway, and the publicity agent, for the region's subsequent rapid development, Lee and other cartoonists played prominent roles.

In 1898 the *Post-Intelligencer* introduced a strip format of cartoons rounding up the previous week's events. These strips were variously called "Pen Record," "Panorama of the Week," and "Happenings of the Week." Other newspapers were also to adopt this format.

At the turn of the century two cartoonists emerged on the Washington newspaper scene, and they were to wield wide influence both in the Northwest and across the nation. They were William Morris of the *Spokane Spokesman-Review* and Edward Reynolds of the *Tacoma Ledger*.

In 1904, a year after it began running front-page editorial cartoons by various artists, the *Spokesman-Review* hired Morris as full-time cartoonist. Then thirty years old, the artist was to remain a fixture on the front page for a decade. As a boy the self-taught artist would throw turnips onto the floor of his home in Utah, in order to sketch them as they fell. Before moving to Spokane in 1901, Morris had drawn a portrait of a murdered black man and sent it to the *Salt Lake Tribune*. The paper accepted the work and ran the drawing with full credit to Morris, and it was soon reprinted by the national magazine *Truth*, which commented that if the victim in fact was so vicious as he was depicted, he justly deserved his fate.

Morris became a spokesman for the *Spokesman-Review* and, when his cartoons were reprinted across America, a cartooning ambassador for Washington state. In June 1913 he left Spokane for New York and its larger audiences.

Edward S. Reynolds began his career as a printer's devil in Riverside, California and later worked as an artist-reporter for several papers in that state. In those days cartoonists had to double as sketch artists, and ofttimes as news or sports reporters as well. When Reynolds began, artwork in newspapers was reproduced by the "chalk-plate" method, a laborious and dusty process where lines were scratched into chalk-covered plates. In 1903 he joined the *Ledger* in Tacoma, and shortly thereafter gained both fame and the nickname "Tige" because of his cartoon mascot and the local baseball association. The Tigers, owned by John S. Baker, had its fortunes chronicled in Reynolds's sports cartoons, and readers

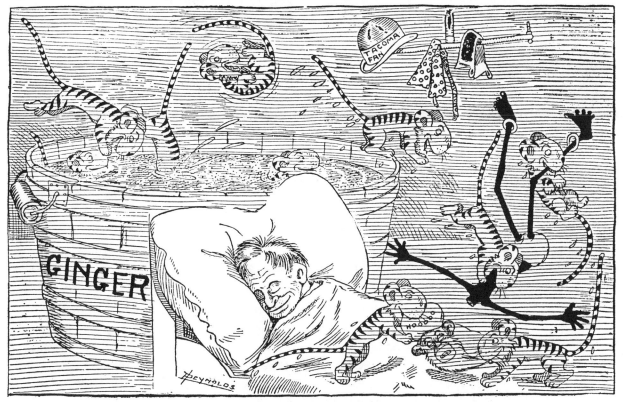

The dream of the Tacoma fan.
Some day he will own a bunch of Tigers with barrels of Ginger.

could instantly learn the outcome of the previous day's game by the expression on Reynolds's tiger in the corner of the cartoon.

Tige Reynolds was remembered as a cheerful man whose retentive memory allowed him to recite poem after poem, and whose musical talents led him to play several instruments, even in the offices of the *Ledger*. In 1911 he left Tacoma to accept a job with the *Portland Oregonian*.

Another local favorite—virtually a legend in Seattle—never gained the national stature of Morris and North, but produced memorable work. John Hager drew all sorts of cartoons but was famed especially for his comic strip, and weather gimcracks, starring Dippy Duck.

"Dok" Hager (who took the nickname because he was a dentist, having only begun car-

tooning while studying dental surgery in Germany) started drawing for the *Seattle Times* in 1905. His weather cartoons paired the duck with an umbrella man, modeled after a local character, a Civil War veteran who wore a silk umbrella canopy over his head as constant protection from the Northwest's drizzles. The cartoon character expanded his observations from weather to all topics, and when the model died in 1913, Dippy Duck moved to center stage and ultimately starred in his own comic strip. The duck typified the Puget Sound resident to whom the rain meant no more discomfort than it did to a duck. Hager continued to draw the front page weather cartoon for nineteen years until he was forced to retire because of failing eyesight.

Two more celebrated cartoonists worked in Seattle during the first two decades of the century: Tom Thurlby and Paul Fung. Thurlby, who was born in England in 1878, had a crippled shoulder since infancy. However, rather than withdraw he worked hard, proving that his handicap was not a hindrance to his development. Not only was he a hard worker but in his youth he was a voracious reader of the classics—history, biography, economics, and current literature.

This early development gave him a strong mind that instantly grasped the fundamentals of every issue. His first newspaper job was with the *Minneapolis Tribune* where his occasional cartoon caught the eye of the Amalgamated Copper Company of Montana. In 1900 he was hired to use his pen against Amalgamated's biggest rival, F. Augustus Heinze.

Several years later he moved to Everett, Washington where he became the editorial writer for the *Everett News*, frequently enlivening the newspaper with his cartoons. While employed in Everett, Thurlby added to his earnings by serving as secretary to Mayor Roland Hartley. The cartoonist even ran the city as acting mayor for four years when the mayor took a leave of absence due to a disability. Later he also worked for the *Seattle Post-Intelligencer* (1910–15) and the *Seattle Times* (1915–28).

Thurlby's cartoons were boldly satirical and had an incisive wit. He drew memorable cartoons, especially during the war years. But the artist also had a tender sentiment which was a keynote of the real Thurlby. When he died at his drawing table in 1928, his death was a loss not only to Seattle but to the Pacific Coast as well.

Born in Seattle in 1897, the son of Chinese missionaries, Paul Fung was schooled in China and trained in Chinese art. But he loved the American comic strips of the Sunday supplements that his sister mailed to China. Back in Seattle, he drew for his high school newspaper and answered an ad from a local theater that needed cartoon lobby cards. His success and notoriety attracted the attention of the *Seattle Post-Intelligencer*, which offered him a job.

For a time Fung played the role of the "only Oriental cartoonist in captivity," but his talent went way beyond the bounds of being a novelty in his chosen profession. He drew political cartoons of great power and superb graphic quality; and with equal success drew weekly bird's-eye views—detailed and hilarious—of local goings-on.

Spring madness is epidemic in houseboat
and bungalow colony on Lake Washington

From the *Post-Intelligencer* he was noticed by the head office of the Hearst newspaper chain, and by the mid 1920s Fung was a cartoonist in New York, ghosting such comic strips as *Barney Google* and *Polly and Her Pals* for their creators, and drawing strips of his own including *Gus and Gussie* and the famous *Dumb Dora* (a phrase that has entered the dictionaries). Fung's son Paul, Jr., also became a cartoonist for Hearst and drew several features, including hundreds of *Blondie* comic books.

The success of these cartoonists assured the employment of more artists to continue the tradition and satisfy the appetite of people in Washington state for daily, local cartoons. In Seattle the work of cartoonists like George Hager, Stuart Morris, and A. R. Slaymaker often appeared on front pages. As issues like labor strife, the social threats of IWW radicalism, a municipal general strike, and the First World War loomed, cartoonists were there to document the events and influence readers.

It was during the First World War that cartoons became highly sophisticated tools of propaganda that promoted support for American men fighting on foreign soil. The public became accustomed to following the war through front page illustrations, often in color. Cartoonists helped galvanize sentiments and loyalties. A majority promoted purchase of war bonds and enlistment, and attempted to instill in citizens a hatred and fear of the enemy. As the war came to a close, cartoonists continued to lure readers with their front-page illustrations about local events.

The influence of the cartoonist in Washington state history is attested to by a campaign of the *Tacoma Ledger*. In what amounted to teasing its readership, the paper ran a large blank space on the front

The winter cache.

page on December 25, 1918. A legend promised readers a Christmas present. All manner of speculation was ended by the announcement that Tige Reynolds was returning to cartoon Washington; it was indeed received as a major, and joyous event.

Although Tige Reynolds was loved by sports enthusiasts, he was essentially a news cartoonist. He cartooned primarily state and national current events, and was considered one of the leaders among West Coast cartoonists. His achievement was to blend the talent of an artist with remarkable news judgment. He had the news of the day at his fingertips and translated his comments into cartoons that were artistically perfect and strikingly effective. With the stroke of a pen he could provoke a laugh or bring a tear. When he died in 1931 from a heart ailment, he drew many a tear from admirers all over the country.

In the 1920s syndication allowed local papers to run the work of the most famous and talented cartoonists from around America. In this way Washingtonians got the opportunity to see the powerful work of such legendary cartoonists as F. Opper, Winsor McCay, and R. W. Satterfield. But homegrown cartoonists continued to work in the Evergreen State, and they attracted loyal corps of followers.

The publisher of the *Seattle Daily Times*, C. B. Blethan, was impressed by the competition's illustrators. Stuart Pratt had been at the *Seattle Post-Intelligencer* for ten years and showed great style as an illustrator and cartoonist. In 1929 the *Times* offered Pratt $5.00 more per week than the *Post-Intelligencer* paid, and so Stuart became a "Timesman." Pratt was a versatile artist who did just about everything well. While at the *Times* he drew editorial, feature, and sports illustrations and cartoons. He was a splendid draftsman with a stylistic brush technique who produced consistently excellent illustrations for news

Joe Louis, by Stuart Pratt

and magazine sections. Especially noteworthy were his color movie promotional drawings for the Sunday entertainment section. His work appeared in the *Times* for more than three decades until his retirement in 1965.

Also in the 1920s the *Seattle Star*, the smallest of Seattle's three daily newspapers, hired a combination artist and police reporter by the name of Sam Groff. He became a rather popular cartoonist during that period, specializing in lampoons of politicians and other public figures. He joined the *Seattle Times* in 1935 after his caricatures of C. B. Blethan won Blethan's admiration. Once again, the publisher offered more money than the *Star* was able to pay, and bought another cartoonist for his paper.

Groff reached the height of his popularity as a cartoonist with his pen-and-ink portrayals of the fortunes and vicissitudes of the Seattle team of the Pacific Coast Baseball League. Everyone in the Northwest knew and enjoyed the amusing adventures of Elmer d'Rainier; Beulah, the beautiful and almost always elusive Coast League championship; Picklepuss; and the other lovable characters Groff created in Seattle baseball.

Although his sports cartoons in the *Times* were well known, he was noted for his cartoon inventions to catch fish. His cartoons followed in the style of Rube Goldberg whose contraptions made for sure catches. For more than a decade Groff's drawings brightened the *Times* sports pages until he died in 1950.

Washington's long history of radicalism and advocacy of progressive causes was mirrored in the 1930s and 1940s in the *New Dealer*, a weekly publication that was later called the *New World*. Walt Partymiller, a University of Washington graduate, moved from drawing cartoons for his college paper and yearbook to this publication. His strong grease-crayon cartoons were in the style and tradition of the great liberal cartoonists like Robert Minor, Boardman Robinson, and D. R. Fitzpatrick. He eventually moved east to become the long-time regular cartoonist of the York (Pa.) *Record*, but Washington papers even then continued to run reprints of the hometown favorite. In the *New Dealer* and the *New World* there also appeared cartoons by local artists like Dave Mero, and national cartoonists like William Gropper.

In the mainstream papers, two talented sons of two famous cartoonists began careers around mid century. Al Pratt was hired by the *Seattle Times* in 1942 when the *Times* lost three of its artists to the Second World War. His father, Stuart Pratt, tried to discourage

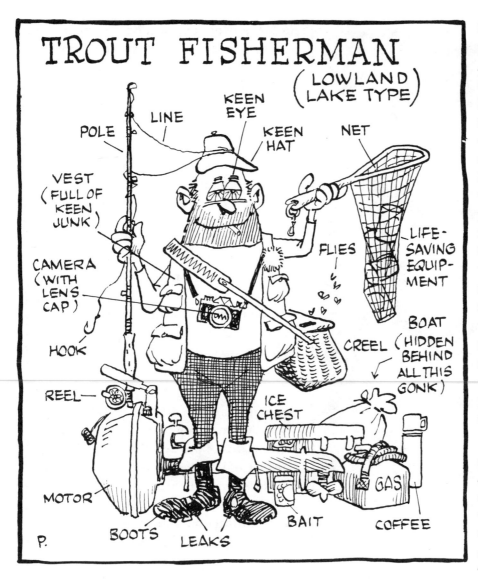

TROUT FISHERMAN (LOWLAND LAKE TYPE)

POLE
LINE
KEEN EYE
KEEN HAT
NET
VEST (FULL OF KEEN JUNK)
FLIES
LIFE-SAVING EQUIPMENT
CAMERA (WITH LENS CAP)
BOAT
CREEL (HIDDEN BEHIND ALL THIS GONK)
HOOK
REEL
ICE CHEST
GAS
MOTOR
BOOTS
LEAKS
BAIT
COFFEE
P.

him from taking the position, but young Al needed a job to support another college year before the army got him. He became chief editorial cartoonist in 1956. He drew political cartoons for many years, but is perhaps most fondly remembered by Washingtonians for his famous and amusing fishing cartoons, which have appeared in all formats from newspaper cartoons to limited-edition prints for compleat anglers.

Shaw McCutcheon's father was John T. McCutcheon. The latter, who worked from his Olympian studio atop the Tribune Towers in Chicago, was for years regarded as the dean of American cartooning. The senior McCutcheon was a winner of multiple Pulitzer prizes. "My father was a cartoonist and used to describe how he became one," McCutcheon remembered. "He was at Purdue University and inquired as to which department required the least amount of math. Someone responded, 'the art department.' He signed up and later became a cartoonist. In my case, I majored in math and later became a cartoonist. This must prove something, but I never have figured out exactly what." For more than thirty-five years, after being hired by the *Spokesman-Review* in 1950, residents of Spokane were grateful that ink flowed through the cartoonist's veins as McCutcheon's handsome and humorous cartoons provided steady commentary and gentle persuasion.

Bob McCausland joined the editorial art staff of the *Post-Intelligencer* in 1945, handling various chores, but it was not until 1959 that he scored his biggest cartooning hit. In that year he created a character called Hairbreadth Husky, the name reminiscent of the old strip character Hairbreadth Harry, but in reality a mascot of the University of Washington football team—slightly underfed, sporting a booster hat, and wearing an oversized letterman's jacket.

Like Tige Reynold's old mascot, one glance at McCausland's Husky could tell the readers how the team had fared. As luck would have it, the first year of the character's appearance the team went to the Rose Bowl. Hairbreadth Husky appeared twice a week (once before and once after each game) for twenty-two years until the cartoonist's retirement.

McCAUSLAND

The renaissance of syndicated political cartoons nationally in the 1960s and 1970s—led by such great talents as Pat Oliphant and Jeff MacNelly—worked against local editorial cartoonists. Papers could contract for a wide range of talent for a fraction of one local artist's salary, and editors could pick and choose from all issues and competing viewpoints. For a time much of the ferment in Washington cartooning switched to "underground" papers, a movement that brought several cartoonists to national prominence. A cult favorite—and, ironically, an inspiration to many underground cartoonists of a later generation—was Basil Wolverton, whose detailed, often bizarre characters ranged from figures in science-fiction comic books to the model for Al Capp's "Lena the Hyena" in *Li'l Abner.* Wolverton later drew Christian comic books.

The *Helix* was Seattle's first underground newspaper. It was begun during the counterculture of the sixties, largely as a response to city prosecutor Charles O. Conner's selective application of what the paper's founders considered to be archaic laws, specifically those relating to free speech. Inspired by the *Berkeley Barb* and *San Francisco Oracle*, *Helix* packaged left-wing politics and counterculture philosophy with lively, often provocative graphics in a multicolor tabloid format, attracting an average weekly circulation of 10,000 copies through June, 1970.

Cartoonists and graphic artists played a major role throughout the life of *Helix*. *Post-Intelligencer* cartoonist Ray Collins, who wanted to name the paper "Peeping Fred" after a flasher then prowling the University of Washington campus, was one of the tabloid's founders.

The work of cartoonists R. Crumb, Ron Cobb, Walt Crowley, Merril Clemmens, Gary Eagle, and Jacque Moitoret all appeared in the *Helix's* pages, and legendary names in underground cartooning circles, like Bobby London, Sharry Flenniken, and Gary Hallgren, all worked in Seattle. As Walt Crowley tells it, most underground newspapers have passed into history, but they left an indelible mark by permanently expanding the boundaries for cartooning and editorial graphics in America's "establishment press."

Out of this movement emerged cartoonists who often addressed social issues rather than political, or at least traditionally partisan, subjects. Matt Groening, whose *Life is Hell* strips have been successfully syndicated and collected in popular books, recently moved from Seattle. Lynda Barry, whose strips and written pieces on female angst in the 1980s have also attracted nationwide acclaim, now divides her time between Seattle and New York.

Possibly the most famous of the local cartoonists is Gary Larson, whose *Far Side* cartoons have enjoyed phenomenal success in American newspapers and bookstores. His bizarre animals and unlikely situations have adorned (through posters, notecards, and calendars) countless refrigerator doors and bulletin boards—and stimulated not a few nightmares.

Peter Bagge is an underground favorite who lives in Seattle. His unorthodox strips have appeared in his own *Neat Stuff* magazine as well as in R. Crumb's *Weirdo* magazine, which Bagge edits. Although he works in Seattle, Michael Dougan is another cult favorite whose main themes are east Texas locales and ways.

Two publishers of comics that specialize in issue-oriented and avant-garde material are located in Seattle. Leonard Rifas is a cartoonist and historian who is publisher of Educomics, which promotes educational, ecological and pacifist issues through cartoons and comic strips. Fantagraphics Books publishes nearly forty different comic titles ranging from reprints of vintage material to underground themes. It also publishes the critical magazines, *The Comics Journal* and *Nemo: The Classic Comics Library*.

Two mainstream comic book artists live in Washington: Mike Grell, whose recent work for DC has included *Green Arrow*; and Steve Gallacci, whose specialty is science fiction featuring half human, half animal characters. There are enough cartooning Washingtonians that a society, Cartoonists Northwest, has formed, with its own newsletter, *Penstuff*. Among members and fellow cartoonists are Diana Babbit, Donna Barr, Jim Blanchard, Mark Campos, Susan Catherine, Bruce Chrislup, Michael Dowers, Tom Grothus, Nils Osmar, John Strongbow and Mark Zingarelli.

Back in the "above ground" domain of mainstream cartoonists on major dailies, Ray Collins held an important post at the *Post-Intelligencer*. Called the "house revolutionary" by fellow workers, he started at the paper in 1949 as a photo retoucher ("drawing arrows to a baby's body and painting the sex organs off animals," he remembered), but eventually earned a spot cartooning on the editorial pages.

In what was perhaps a cosmic updating of Dok's *Dippy Duck*, Collins's popular creation was *Cecil C. Addle*, featuring Dipstick, a black saltwater duck that represented unorthodox and sometimes unpopular viewpoints. The strip's formula presented an invariable oppressor, Cecil or Dipstick as victims, and the Log—a place for rational retreat. One of Collins's favorite targets was Governor Dixy Lee Ray who often pushed commerce over conservation. Her efforts to allow supertankers on Puget Sound was ridiculed by cartoonists throughout the state.

During his college years David Horsey cartooned for the *University of Washington Daily*. After graduation in 1976 he moved his pen to the *Journal-American*, where he also worked as a political reporter. Horsey began to syndicate his cartoons to approximately fifteen papers statewide before being hired by the *Post-Intelligencer* in 1979, just about the time that Ray Collins retired.

Horsey was a finalist for the Pulitzer Prize in 1987. His cartoons have an important element of caricature and favor the scalpel over the hatchet when dissecting an issue. Horsey's cartoons are syndicated to more than three hundred newspapers across the North America, and he also drew a comic strip, *Boomer's Song*, from 1986 to 1989.

Horsey's roots as a cartoonist go back before college. In the late 1960s he had cartooned for the Ingraham High School *Cascade*, a nationally acclaimed student newspaper that also helped train Steve McKinstry. McKinstry was a local artist who worked briefly for the *Seattle Times* and *Post-Intelligencer* before moving with his pen to various cities around the nation.

Another University of Washington cartoonist graduate, and finalist for the Pulitzer Prize in 1986, was Mike Lukovich. Lukovich moved around a lot as a child and used cartoons as a way of making friends. "The other kids enjoyed the way I could draw funny pictures of the teachers and make it look like them." In college while drawing for the *University of Washington Daily* (1978-1982) he recognized the power of cartooning and how his cartoons could affect the way people thought.

After graduation, Lukovich sent résumés to almost every newspaper in the country, hoping to land a job as a cartoonist. While he waited, he resorted to what he considers the world's worst occupation—selling life insurance. Finally he convinced the Greenville, North Carolina *News* and later the New Orleans *Times Picayune* that he was a better cartoonist than an insurance salesman. Lukovich sees cartooning as therapy. He is able to channel his frustrations with the political process, the neglect of the environment, and the silliness of the world's leaders into a cartoon.

Another editorial cartoonist doubling as a strip cartoonist is also, in what is becoming a Washington tradition, the son of another famous cartoonist. Brian Basset is the son of Gene Basset, whose many years of cartooning included political work for the *Washington News* in Washington, D.C. and the Scripps-Howard chain. Brian became editorial cartoonist for the *Seattle Times* in 1978 after graduating from Ohio State University; his popular strip about the life of a house-husband is called *Adam*. About the practice of attacking and lampooning institutions in his political cartoons, Basset has written, "Contrary to the segment of the population who believe I can be the desecrator of our state and the nation, I chuckle and remind myself why I do what I do. It's because I have the highest regard for the Constitution and I cherish our freedom of speech and expression."

Another cartoonist for a major daily in the state, Milt Priggee of Spokane's *Spokesman-Review* and *Chronicle*, seems to be a man on a mission. As he tells it, if he sees an injustice, he wants to bring attention to it in order to stir up a debate: "Cartoonists are paid to reveal the awkward truth when all others would prefer a tactful silence." He believes that a cartoonist should be biased and take one side or the other: "There are only two sides to an issue—the wrong side and the cartoonist's side." Of course, sometimes his editors disagree with that philosophy. According to Priggee, he has complete freedom to draw anything he wants, and his editors have complete freedom to reject anything that he draws.

Political cartooning is not the sole domain of the major dailies. Although most small papers are unable to afford a full-time cartoonist, their readers are able to enjoy the wit and creative talent of Frank Shiers. Shiers, represented by the T. R. Syndicate in western Washington, addresses many Washington political and social issues.

Shiers's work appears in eight weeklies and seven dailies. His work is almost as identifiable to as many people in the state as is that of cartoonists for the major dailies. He enjoys his role as "small town cartoonist." He says it's like having his own letter to the editor published twice a week. He knows that his cartoons will often be read by elected officials and takes great pride in knowing that he can have an effect on policy-makers. In the words of H. L. Mencken, he likes to "comfort the afflicted and afflict the comfortable."

And there are many more artists who have cartooned Washington. The state's motto *Alki* (Chinook for "by and by"), does not apply to cartooning in Washington during the Evergreen State's first one hundred years. Numerous cartoonists have been in the forefront of major events and issues. Washington has had its crowded hours, with a lot to note in its first century—and cartoonists have been the note-takers, prodding and exhorting along the way.

And here is their record.

Maury Forman
Rick Marschall

1889–1899

North Dakota, South Dakota, Montana, Washington.
—Admitted into the Union, February 22nd, 1889.

The Debut of the Younger Sisters

March 1889

C. J. Taylor

Puck

The Admission of Wash.

November 23, 1889

C. Lamb

West Shore

Washington statehood was initially proposed in 1878. The voters approved the state constitution, but Congress failed to pass it. One of the major reasons for this defeat concerned a question of territorial boundaries involving eastern Oregon and the Idaho panhandle. Another reason was solely political. The Democrats controlled Congress at the time and they feared that once Washington became a state its new citizens would send Republicans to Congress.

In 1888 Republican Benjamin Harrison was elected president and his party gained control of Congress. An "enabling" act was passed, and on November 11, 1889 President Harrison signed the proclamation making Washington the forty-second state admitted to the union. Elisha P. Ferry—a Republican—was voted to be the first governor.

Puck magazine, America's oldest and largest political-humor weekly, ran this double-page cartoon spread celebrating the entrance of Washington and her sister territories into the Union. The cartoonist was C. J. Taylor, a respected illustrator and cartoonist, who was more known for his pen-and-ink work (this is a lithograph) and society drawings. Perhaps this is a reason why he chose to depict the established states as society ladies at a "coming out" party and the territories as frontier types. Most likely such a depiction fit in with Easterners' conceptions of the American West. Note the figure of Canada in the distance—"out in the cold"— because it coveted the territories itself, or perhaps because it, too, secretly wished to be part of the Union. Less elegant cartoonists, like C. Lamb, used the occasion of statehood to reach for a cheap pun—"The Admission of Wash." The latter approach is as much the domain of the cartoonist as a profound statement or a historical observation.

The State of Washington extending her cordial welcome to
James J. Hill and his Great Northern Railway and inviting them to partake of her wealth. He
exclaims: "What! All this?"

"What! All This?"

March 24, 1893

Unknown

New West

By the time Washington became a state, James J. Hill's Great Northern Railway was
making its way to Puget Sound. In 1890 Hill chose Seattle as the railroad's western
terminus and began laying tracks from the east that would bring growth and new
business for thge whole area. Hill lured both Americans and immigrants to the West with
discount fares, and he even offered a "good for one year" three thousand-mile ticket for
seventy-five dollars. On January 6, 1893, a spike joined the Great Northern's east and
west lines, and in July the first Great Northern transcontinental train came into Seattle.

"Mr. Villard is going abroad, it is reported, to stay an indefinite time. He goes with full pockets, but he leaves behind him empty treasuries. His career has been unique. With no ostensible or visible occupation for the past five years, other than that of president or chairman of three great companies, he leaves them impoverished, but he has acquired a fortune, if his friends' statements can be trusted, at the rate of a million a year. His active brain and his skillful diplomacy contributed chiefly to the success of the effort to fasten on the Northern Pacific the burdens of the Wisconsin Central. A more flagrant breach of trust and a more shameless disregard of the duties of trustees and directors have not been seen in the history of American railroads.—*President Brayton Ives.*

Villard, like the Phœnix, rises rejuvenated from the
wreck of the Northern Pacific Railroad.

The Champion Railroad Wrecker

October 28, 1893
Unknown
New West

One of the most prominent and hated figures in early state history was journalist-turned-financier Henry Villard. In 1881 Villard gained the presidency of the Northern Pacific, and for the next two years worked to complete the first northern transcontinental railroad. On September 8, 1883 Villard himself drove the golden spike that linked rail lines from St. Paul, Minnesota to Kalama, Washington along the Columbia River. Subsequently the main line was built across the Cascades from Pasco to Auburn and on into Seattle.

Previously Tacoma had been slated to become the western terminus, and Tacomans and their papers, including the *New West,* considered Villard a crook for taking the honor and potential economic benefits away from them.

"Beware, little girl; he ruined me."

Warning of the Ghost of Kansas

September 27, 1896

Unknown

Seattle Post Intelligencer

Dr. Roger's Populist Cure-all

October 1, 1896

Unknown

Seattle Post-Intelligencer

Reform movements were stirring up change in Washington during the 1890s and the Populist Party found widespread acceptance at the ballot box during this decade. The Democratic Party had insulated itself from new ideas and soon found its party faithful moving over to the Populists. The *Post-Intelligencer* ran its first cartoon campaign, urging citizens to beware of populist promises and self-interest. These cartoons often used "Death" and the Kansas populist experience to create fear in the voter. In Kansas Populists were elected in the 1892 election, but after the Depression hit in 1893 their programs failed to help the economy.

In 1896, despite the negative press, Washington became one of only three states to elect a Populist governor. In electing John R. Rogers of Puyallup, Washingtonians were endorsing a child's right to a public education, lower railroad and utility rates, a bimetallic standard for the nation's currency reserves (at a 16-to-1 silver-to-gold ratio), a state income tax, and direct election of United States Senators.

Rogers had been an adept journalist and legislator, but because of Populist infighting many of his reforms never became law. By the end of his first term many of Rogers's ideas were moving into the political mainstream and were endorsed by Democrats. The Klondike gold rush also refocused the public's attention, and the momentum of populism waned. In fact, Rogers was reelected as a Democrat. He died in office and was succeeded by Henry McBride—a Republican.

The State of Washington: "No, I thank you Doctor.
Your quack remedies have proved to be too dangerous."

(Captions for frames 1, 2, 4, 5, 6:)
Which road shall they chose? — What they all crave for. — Now an even swap. —
"Hot time in the old town" — First call for dinner.

Klondiker Gold Rush

July 18, 1897
A. H. Lee
Seattle Post-Intelligencer

A Klondiker's Dream

August 22, 1897
Unknown
Seattle Post-Intelligencer

Washington's answer to its economic depression came in the form of gold that was discovered more than fifteen hundred miles away in Alaska's Klondike territory. Although no gold was found in Seattle, the city conducted a public relations coup by promoting Seattle as the "Gateway to the Gold." People from all over the country assisted in the area's economic recovery by stopping in Seattle to buy merchandise and food before moving on to the Klondike. Cartoonist Lee provided weekly strips that linked Alaska's discovery with the glories of the Northwest.

Another cartoonist, whose identity is lost to history, made a social and even moralistic comment in a time when many newspaper cartoons were either purely humorous or savagely political. Here is sentiment alone and a tender exception to the hoopla surrounding the gold rush. Many individuals and shops in Washington were prospering as thousands sought provisions for the rush north. However this cartoonist chooses to remember the regrettable underside of the glamour: the family left behind, the hardships, and the loneliness. The drawing proves that there can be greater poetry in a sensitive cartoon than in rhymed lines.

He forgot for a moment the hunger and cold.
The weakness, the longing and fierce racking pain.
And his soul loosed its grip on the dearly bought gold.
And away from the storms over mountain and plain.
It sped to the sunshine, to the love and to life;
To color and beauty, to child and wife.
—J.A. Kempster.

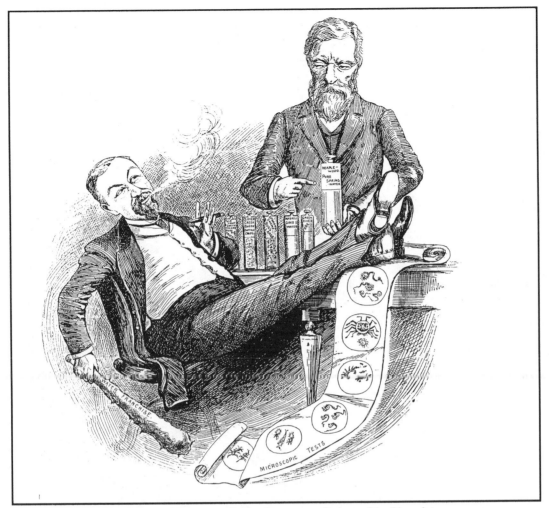

Hosmer—I guess we'll take Spanaway Swamp, Mr. Chemist.
Yaas, the bugs are big and the slime is pretty thick and the taste is a little off, but its
good enough for Tacoma. Then it comes so much cheaper for the "old man."
The bigger the "old man's" profits, the bigger my salary is. See?
Chemist—But here is the pure thing from Maplewood Springs, and the people demand pure water.
Hosmer—Oh, that purchase was made just to quiet'em.

Hosmer Receiving the Chemist's Report

December 2, 1892
Unknown
New West

Theodore Hosmer was manager of the Tacoma Land Co. and also an officer of the privately owned Tacoma Light and Water Co. This cartoon from the front page of the *New West* depicts Hosmer deceiving Tacomans into drinking bad water and making them pay a price five times as high as Tacoma's northern neighbors. It was this cartoon that helped expose the corruption in the water company. Eventually the City of Tacoma took the water company to court for not fulfilling the terms of its franchise. In 1898 Tacoma, by order of the court, purchased Tacoma Light and Water Co., thus making Tacoma the first large city in the state to produce its own power.

It may have been everybody's pig, but it is now Olympia's bacon.

The Boss Dog Carries the Bone

March 17, 1893
Unknown
New West

There was much for cities to howl about after the 1893 legislative session. Government financial resources were as scarce one hundred years ago as they are today, and cities had to compete to get building appropriations. In 1893 legislators allocated most available money to Olympia so that the state could begin constructing its capitol. The first capitol was located in downtown Olympia in a building now occupied by the offices of the Superintendent of Public Instruction.

Ashes to Ashes, Dust to Dust

February 14, 1897

A. H. Lee

Seattle Post-Intelligencer

This cartoon parodies the state's first scandal in the legislature and mocks how the legislature covered it up. Before passage of the Seventeenth Amendment to the United States Constitution, state legislators elected U.S. senators. On January 28, 1897 the *Post-Intelligencer* made charges of foul play and corruption in the election of Judge George Turner for the U.S. Senate. Under pressure from the public and newspaper cartoonists a legislative investigation ensued. Nearly one-third of the state's senators and representatives were accused of offering or taking bribes for votes. On February 9 the investigative committee found that no one was guilty beyond a reasonable doubt.

1900–1909

Inside the cartoon: President Hill of the Great Northern in an interview declares if the suit begun by the Harriman interests is successful he will retire, and says that if the Northern Pacific goes into the hands of hostile interests he has fought his last battle for the Northwest.

A Head On Collision!

April 18, 1904

James North

Tacoma Daily News

James J. Hill, president of the Great Northern Railway and later the Northern Pacific Railway, was the only man who built a transcontinental railroad without a subsidy or land grant from the federal government. When E. H. Harriman, president of the Union Pacific Railroad, challenged Hill's railroad dominance in the Northwest, a major court battle took place in 1904. Hill declared that if the suit was successful, he would retire and leave the Northwest. In 1905 the Supreme Court sided with Hill and blocked Harriman's attempt to force his way into the area. Hill stayed and as James North illustrated, the lawyers got rich.

What One Santa Claus Will Give

December 20, 1905

George Hager

Seattle Post-Intelligencer

At Christmas time in 1905 James J. Hill presented to leaders around the world boxes of Washington's now famous apples. The *Post-Intelligencer* reported each apple to be "large and juicy and perfectly formed." These gifts from Hill not only served to advertise a Washington product but reminded world figures of the immense spoils that had become part of Hill's empire. Cartoonist Hager could not resist dressing the rotund Hill in a Santa Claus outfit.

MT. WHITNEY—They say that I'm the highest mountain in the country.
MT. RAINIER—Don't mind that; some people even say that my name is "Mt. Tacoma."

I'm The Highest Mountain

September 19, 1905
George Hager
Seattle Post-Intelligencer

A Great Sight

August 1, 1908
James North
Tacoma Daily News

Throughout Washington state's history the cartoonist never dallied when joining the battle to protect his community's interest and pride. One of the longest running cartoon battles was penned over the name for Mt. Rainier—or is it Mt. Tacoma? In these two cartoons George Hager leads the campaign for Seattleites, and James North for Tacomans.

Capt. George Vancouver of the British Royal Navy named Mt. Rainier in 1792 in honor of his friend, Rear Adm. Peter Rainier. The name "Takhoma" is native American in origin, and although it is generally thought to be the name native Americans gave to the mountain, its precise meaning is uncertain. According to professor of history Arthur D. Martinson, it was not until the 1860s that "Takhoma" or "Tahoma" became widely known to early Puget Sound settlers. It was the coming of the railroad, however, that finally made the mountain's name controversial.

The Northern Pacific Railroad officially declared the mountain "Tacoma" in a publication in 1883, and the battle began. Seattle citizens were outraged that the mountain's historical name could be stolen, and Tacomans retorted that "Rainier" was un-American. Besides, Tacomans would claim, what right did George Vancouver have to name everything in sight?

Decades passed, and even presidents took sides. Theodore Roosevelt, William Taft, and Woodrow Wilson supported "Mt. Tacoma." The United States Board of Geographic Names continually supported "Mt. Rainier." The board members were accused of being bribed by a well-known Seattle brewery, but the Board's opinion, and perhaps taste, stayed the same.

In 1925 the Congressional Committee on Public Lands voted *against* a resolution to change the name from "Rainier" to "Tacoma." Finally in 1939 the Tacoma Chamber of Commerce passed a resolution asking that all Tacomans accept the name Mt. Rainier. Although it may seem like this battle is over, one cartoon could start the controversy rumbling again.

President Roosevelt: "You are a fine, sturdy fellow,
but you need a little polish."

Football Polish

October 11, 1905

William C. Morris

Spokesman-Review

The first football game between the University of Washington and the Washington Agricultural College (now Washington State University) was played in 1900. Football players back then wore no helmets, an offensive player could move a defensive player out of the way by any means possible, and the game was longer. There were also fewer officials, substitutions were prohibited, and teams played more than one game a week. These old "rules" resulted in many deaths and permanent injuries.

The violence prompted Pres. Theodore Roosevelt to call a conference in October 1905 that would forever change collegiate football. Innovations that eventually resulted from this conference attended by football "experts" included reducing game time from 70 to 60 minutes, legalizing the forward pass, forbidding hurdling, increasing officials from three to four, requiring football gear, giving the offense only four downs to make ten yards, changing the touchdown points from four to six and field goals from five to three, and forming the National Collegiate Athletic Association.

Mayor Daggett and His Platform

April 21, 1907
William C. Morris
Spokesman-Review

In 1907 Democratic Mayor Floyd L. Daggett of Spokane ran for reelection with a "leave well enough alone" platform. Besides Daggett's permissive police policy towards vice and tolerance of minors in saloons, his platform promised continued support of a new water system, construction of a municipal lighting plant, and new bridges. As Daggett campaigned, he spoke of how well Spokane was policed and how certain evils were better regulated in Spokane than in any other Washington city.

Cartoonist William Morris did not buy Daggett's rhetoric. To Morris, Daggett's platform was basically supported by the dives around town. Morris recalled (and virtually copied) the depiction of a malefactor's hand in this cartoon from the powerful work of William Randolph Hearst's chief cartoonist at the time, Homer Davenport. Davenport's hoary hands were usually attached to figures of trusts and monopolists.

That May many Democrats were reelected, but Spokane overwhelmingly elected Dagett's Republican opponent, Herbert Moore, as mayor.

She Likes It

April 24, 1907
William C. Morris
Spokesman-Review

In March 1907 the Washington state legislature passed the "direct primary" law. The law provided for candidates to be nominated by the people, not party bosses, in an election prior to the general election. Many citizens supported this law because unpopular incumbents, such as Mayor Daggett of Spokane, were not guaranteed a place on the general election ballot. The new law was also very specific on how elections in the state were to be conducted.

"Now if you men will give me elbow room, I'll show you
how to transact business."

The Women's Clubs Convention

May 28, 1907

William C. Morris

Spokesman-Review

What originally began as a literary club, formed for social companionship and
self-cultivation, grew into a federation of clubs to help others. In May 1907 the
Washington State Federation of Women's Clubs held its eleventh convention in Spokane.
Ninety-four different clubs were represented at that convention, and it was attended by
two hundred delegates. As a greeting, Spokane stores arranged display windows in the
Federation colors of green and white.

The convention sessions held at the Masonic Temple were open to the public. The delegates
passed many significant measures during the course of a week, taking positions on judicial
and election reform, education, protection of forests, and other subjects. The most raucous
moment of the convention came when Seattle Police Chief Wappenstein slurred club women
by saying, "Boys that go wrong, do so because their mothers are too busy with clubs and
not at home." The Federation decided it was below its dignity to respond officially to him.
Ironically, Wappenstein was later caught in a vice scandal.

Pinched!

June 19, 1907

William C. Morris

Spokesman-Review

The Spokane drug store owner in William C. Morris's cartoon has reason to cry because Police Chief Rice has just put a kibosh on a lot of his business. Drug stores had been attracting a large audience by adding an intoxicating "stick" into temperance drinks. Although there were many temperance supporters in Washington, Spokane city officials were not concerned about the liquor in drinks. The officials were more concerned about unfair competition with the saloons. The city fathers decided to stop the "sticking" unless drug stores got a retail liquor license just like the saloons.

Cleaning Week in Spokane

May 15 , 1909
William C. Morris
Spokesman-Review

Communities pull together in times of natural disaster, and today we are used to reading about civic cooperation after floods and hurricanes. Beginning in March 1909 the disaster was a scarlet fever epidemic which hit the Spokane area. The health department was put on twenty-four-hour alert, cleaning up refuse and inspecting school children. Children were not permitted to play together, patients were quarantined up to six weeks, and in at least one case, an entire train was quarantined when an escaped patient boarded in Coeur d'Alene.

Spokane's hilly topography kept the disease east of Hangman Creek. Citizens rallied with "cleaning weeks," and cases of the fever decreased. By the beginning of June the health department was able to reduce its forces.

Uncle Sam: "Well! well! a world's fair away out here in Seattle! It seems but yesterday that my sloop of war, the Decatur, was shelling the Indians and saving the settlers here."

Welcome

June 1, 1909
George Hager
Seattle Post-Intelligencer

Uncle Sam: Well! Well!

June 2, 1909
William C. Morris
Spokesman-Review

The Alaska-Yukon-Pacific Exposition of 1909 was held in Seattle, commemorating Washington's astonishing growth and prominence in only twenty years as a state. The name and site were chosen because of the role of the Gold Rush in the vitality of the region, and Seattle's role in the Gold Rush. The fair became a larger celebration of the entire Pacific Rim's expansion. Professor Edmond Meany was instrumental in getting the fair on the University of Washington campus.

On June 1, opening day, railroad magnate James J. Hill enthusiastically addressed the crowd: "The future belongs to you . . . you can indulge in no ambition too high, no faith too certain, no hope too great. You will never again know isolation." Banker and exposition president J. E. Chilberg welcomed exhibitors from as far away as New York and the Philippines, and more than 3.5 million people attended the fair. It attracted such notables as President Taft, William Jennings Bryan, foreign ambassadors, and eight state governors.

Let Us Hope For the Best

July 3, 1909
James North
Tacoma Daily News

The Fourth of July — Safe, Sane, and Otherwise

July 2, 1916
Paul Fung
Seattle Post-Intelligencer

A "safe and sane Fourth" was a yearly campaign to keep children from killing themselves and others with fireworks that started early in Washington history. The sane Fourth talk dated back to the beginnings of American history. The first advocate was Lord George Cornwallis who made great concessions to abate the American celebration at Yorktown.

The editor of the Seattle *Weekly Tribune*, Thomas Prosch, initiated the "Sane Fourth of July" movement bill for the area in 1876 after reporting about it during a visit to San Francisco. After consulting with the town marshal, Prosch discovered an ordinance against the reckless discharge of firecrackers and dropped his campaign. For decades, however, the cartoonist's pen acted as a reminder that fireworks and small children do not mix.

He Hates to Let Go

May 14, 1909

William C. Morris

Spokesman-Review

Arraigned

August 13, 1909

Ed "Tige" Reynolds

Tacoma Daily Ledger

Don't Let Him Get Out, Shep

August 18, 1909

Ed "Tige" Renolds

Tacoma Daily Ledger

Washington state was still young when one of its public officials was put on trial for extortion and graft. On June 25, 1909, the state House of Representatives presented to the Senate twenty-six articles of impeachment against Washington insurance commissioner, John H. Schively. Schively's trial lasted until August 26.

The impeachment articles presented against Schively included: charging out-of-state insurance companies admittance fees of two hundred dollars more than the thirty-five dollars required by law and then pocketing the extra money; arbitrarily charging insurance companies examination fees in excess of expenses incurred by Schively; and committing perjury before a grand jury.

Each of the articles of impeachment was voted on separately, and to find Schively guilty a two-thirds vote of the Senate was necessary. John H. Schively was acquitted on all articles. Only a cartoonist's pen could convict him.

1910–1919

She'll Clean 'Em Out

October 24, 1910

Votta

Seattle Star

Where Gill Proudly Stands

January 22, 1911

Hop

Seattle Post-Intelligencer

Hiram Gill was elected mayor of Seattle in 1910 because he believed in the basic tenet of "live and let live." In Seattle at the turn of the century that meant an open town, a town full of gambling and prostitution. Seattle wanted to party, twenty-four hours a day, seven days a week, and Gill and his police chief, Charles W. Wappenstein (Wappy) became the hosts.

What finally did Gill in was building a five-hundred room brothel—using city property. This was too much for local preachers and press. The *Post-Intelligencer* spearheaded a successful recall drive and in February 1911, with women voting for the first time since Washington had become a state, Hiram Gill became the first public figure in the United States to be kicked out of office.

Gill, however, was a resilient politician, and he also wanted to be remembered favorably. In 1914 he ran on a closed town platform—and won. He was reelected in 1916.

And Georgiana Did

December 6, 1910
Unknown
Seattle Star

When Spokane Women Go to Register

Circa 1910
William C. Morris
Spokesman-Review

A Movement Afoot to Instruct Women

November 12, 1910
William C. Morris
Spokesman-Review

In 1972 Washington state voters approved an equal rights amendment to the state constitution, reaffirming the state's commitment to equality between the sexes. However, the battle for sexual equality in this state has not always been easy. Altough the territorial legislature granted women the right to vote in 1883, this right was not extended when the state constitution was adopted.

May Arkwright Hutton, a mining millionaire and Spokane activist, put her energies into the suffrage struggle. West of the Cascades, Emma Smith Devoe, president of the Washington Equal Suffrage Association, led the battle for the ballot. In 1910 the state constitution was amended, and Washington became the fifth state to give women the right to vote. Washington was also the fifth state to ratify the Nineteenth Amendment to the United States Constitution.

The Biggest Boy in School

November 28, 1910

Unknown

Seattle Star

Spokane Enters the 100,000 League

December 10, 1910

William C. Morris

Spokesman-Review

What makes these two cartoons fascinating is that they offer an East/West perspective about the same topic—population growth. Even back then competition was furious between the two sides of the Cascades. Of course, the *Seattle Star* focuses on "Big Boy" Seattle. After the 1910 census Seattle became the twenty-first largest city in the country, ranking ahead of Indianapolis, Denver, and St. Paul. Seattle gained from 80,671 in 1900 to 237,194 in 1910, an increase of 194 percent. Only Birmingham, Alabama and

Los Angeles had gained more. Also noteworthy in this cartoon is that Tacoma is drawn bigger than "Little School Boy" Spokane.

In William C. Morris's cartoon, Spokane does not stand in awe of anyone. She is glamorous as Uncle Sam introduces her to the Society of Cities. As Spokane joins the One Hundred Thousand League, note that Tacoma enviously looks on. Which city was bigger in 1910, Spokane or Tacoma? The Morris cartoon tells it like it was. Tacoma officials originally claimed to have 116,000 people, but the Census Bureau suggested that these numbers were "padded." Although furious over the accusation, Tacoma submitted to a recount. The population of Tacoma in 1910 officially became 83,743, and it would have to wait to be escorted by Uncle Sam.

"The labels of many of these so-called cures indicated
their use for diseases of children. If any of these statements had been true no one with access to
the remedies which bore them need have died from any cause other than accident or old age."
—President Taft, in his message to congress urging amendments to pure food and drugs bill.

If the Truth Were Known

June 23, 1911

William C. Morris

Spokesman-Review

Calling in a doctor was too expensive for many parents, and they often turned to the
cheap bottled remedy to help their ailing children. Although parents believed the
advertising of these cure-alls, their children often died instead of getting better. Although
the Pure Food and Drug Act passed in 1906, it took a potent antidote, like this William C.
Morris cartoon, to help convince Congress in 1911 that it should pass a law making the
use false or misleading labels illegal.

Another Stronghold Falls

November 7, 1914
Herbert Hodges
Spokesman-Review

The state had to be weaned off barleycorn. This cartoon by Herbert Hodges of the *Spokesman-Review* was drawn the day after a statewide initiative passed (Seattle voted against it), preventing the manufacture and sale of all liquor in the state except by druggists; but it also permitted anyone to import liquor from outside the state for private use. This, as Roger Sale remarked in *Seattle, Past to Present*, "kept the wealthy quiet while forcing everyone else to dry up." In 1916 Washington voters approved a referendum that made selling or drinking liquor unlawful. The national prohibition act, also known as the Volstead Act, made the whole country dry in 1920, and the Puget Sound became a rumrunner's paradise.

The Weather

February 1, 1916

John "Dok" Hager

Seattle Daily Times

For years John "Dok" Hager drew daily weather cartoons for the front page of the *Seattle Daily Times*. It was while taking postgraduate dental work in Germany that "Dok", who had always been a dabbler at caricature, studied this form of art closely. His cartoons always featured the Umbrella Man and was patterned after a real Civil War veteran, Robert Patten, who was a familiar figure on the city streets. The Umbrella Man, like Patten, wore a silk umbrella canopy over his grayed locks as protection against Seattle's dismal weather. The Umbrella Man in Dok's strip was the kindly commentator on weather and current topics, embodying the artist's observation of what was going on as well as delivering his philosophies of life. In this cartoon Dok comments on the worst January snowfall in more than two decades—twenty-nine inches.

Self Protection

November 7, 1916
Tom Thurlby
Seattle Daily Times

The Industrial Workers of the World (IWW or Wobblies) were frequently a subject for cartoonists. The Wobblies first organized in 1905 and set the goal of having all American workers in one big union. The Wobblies felt that street speeches, strikes, and sabotage were three methods that would bring about better working conditions; however, these methods also caused many communities to organize citizen armies against them. Everett was one such community.

In November 1916 Everett mill workers were trying to free themselves from the grip of lumber barons, and the Wobblies began to make street speeches to convince Everett citizens that the millworkers were right. Several Wobblies were arrested and then beaten and whipped. Outraged by these events, more than two hundred Wobblies boarded the ship *Verona* on November 5 to hold a protest rally at the city dock. When they arrived, the Wobblies were met by the Everett citizen army. A gun battle ensued and five Wobblies and two Everett citizens were killed. At least fifty others were wounded. Following this "Everett Massacre," seventy-five Wobblies were arrested and charged with murder. No Everett citizen was arrested. The Wobblies were eventually acquitted, but this Thurlby cartoon reflects the growing hatred of communities toward the IWW.

Letting Him Down Easy

Circa 1919

Paul Fung

Seattle Post-Intelligencer

About Time, Isn't It?

November 29, 1916

Hal Coffman

Seattle Daily Times

And In The Meantime

May 21, 1917

R.W. Satterfield

Seattle Star

While men fought the Kaiser in the First World War, women in Washington and all states were called to enlist in the fight against the "Food Speculator." Until May, 1917, food speculators were profiteering from the war by hoarding goods and then charging consumers exorbitant prices. President Wilson and his food administrator, Herbert Hoover, pledged to control food distribution and fix prices. However, the most effective war against the food hog was waged at the local level.

The *Seattle Star* and two hundred other newspapers around the country organized "The Woman's Army Against Waste." The *Star* even had a waste editor, Runabel Abbott. "Waste No Food" became the battle cry. Citizens sent in enlistment cards, and from those, neighborhood meetings were set up to devise methods for conserving food. A concerned public became educated. It was estimated in 1917 that three-quarters of a billion dollars worth of food was being wasted in this country.

We're Ready, Mr. M'Adoo

September, 25, 1918

Paul Fung

Seattle Post-Intelligencer

Lend Power to His Thrust

October 13, 1918

Stuart Morris

Seattle Post-Intelligencer

During the First World War, United States Treasury Secretary William G. McAdoo appealed to the patriotism of Americans through their pocketbooks. A great war, he suggested, must be supported at the grassroots level; taxation was not the answer—at first. Instead, McAdoo led four Liberty Loan campaigns before the armistice, asking citizens and businesses to buy bonds. He enlisted celebrities like Douglas Fairbanks and Mary Pickford to rally support for these campaigns.

In October 1919 the fourth Liberty Loan drive in the State of Washington was an emotional one. Bond quotas were set at every governmental jurisdiction level from state to county to city. Even businesses were given a quota to meet.

When an organization faltered newspapers reported the fact. The Seattle Police Department was called a "bond slacker" at one time because fewer than half of the force had purchased bonds. With six days remaining to the fourth Liberty Loan campaign, it was feared that the drive in Washington would fail. The Seattle/King County area alone was $8 million short of its quota. An "eleventh hour" mass advertising blitz proved successful, and Seattle raised more than $27 million dollars; the state as a whole raised $58 million.

The New Champ

October 13, 1918

Paul Fung

Seattle Post-Intelligencer

> "I had a little bird named 'Enza.'
> I opened the window and in-flu-enza."

The Spanish Influenza began as a joke topic in October 1918 and ended up killing half a million people in the United States and twenty million people worldwide. Besides the familiar sight of white masks worn by citizens in public, and the personal tragedy suffered by many Washingtonians, sports fans endured a lost season. Boxing, bowling, billiards, baseball, football, and soccer were banned. In fact, it was fear of influenza germs that got the spitball banned from baseball. In boxing, even the big fight between Kruvosky and Mickey King was postponed; and after waiting for the epidemic to disappear, officials were forced to cancel the championship game of the Puget Sound Shipyard League. The one sport that seemed to have survived the punch of that fall influenza was golf, and the Jefferson Park links found itself busy with a lot of newcomers. Cartoonist Paul Fung commented on the flu's effect on sports and daily life in general.

Will Tacoma Now Open the Door

November 1, 1918
Sam Armstrong
Tacoma News Tribune

While the influenza epidemic was still taking its toll, citizens of Greater Tacoma rallied in November 1918 and voted to establish a port commission. Strong supporters of the commission were the Northern Pacific shopmen who knew that more ships coming to port would eventually mean more work for them as well. For Tacomans, opportunity knocked, and they answered.

The boys in France by their valor have ended the war—
Will we desert them now or will we furnish them with every comfort
until they come home?

He Has Earned It Over There

November 14, 1918
Sam Armstrong
Tacoma News Tribune

Even as the ink was drying on the Armistice ending the First World War, another campaign was launched by President Wilson to support the troops materially and morally while they remained in Europe. The fund drive for the United War Work of Tacoma and Pierce County made great efforts to reach its quota—originally $181,000, which increased to $240,000 when Wilson asked all organizations to oversubscribe. What made this fundraiser particularly difficult was the influenza ban on large gatherings which continued until the last days of the campaign. Starting on November 14, 1918, the *Tacoma News Tribune* contributed the publicity to help make the effort successful. This Sam Armstrong cartoon was part of the *News Tribune's* campaign.

The State Mourns

June 14, 1919
Sam Armstrong
Tacoma News Tribune

A fine tribute was paid to Gov. Ernest Lister in this Sam Armstrong cartoon published on the day of his death in 1919. Lister's genius for organization guided him to numerous political accomplishments, including administering the draft in this state during the First World War, establishing closer affiliations among northwestern states, and developing a program for the reconstruction work of the nation. When Lister was first elected Governor in 1912 and then reelected in 1916 he was the only Democrat elected to statewide office.

The Awakening

November 13, 1919

Tom Thurlby

Seattle Daily Times

On November 11, 1919, the first anniversary of the end of the First World War, war veterans were parading through Centralia. IWW headquarters were along the parade route and local Wobblies had armed themselves because of earlier attacks against the IWW office. What happened as the parade passed headquarters is still unclear, but gun fire was exchanged and four veterans were killed. Forty-two Wobblies were arrested. One member, Wesley Everest, was taken from his cell that night and lynched. Four other Wobblies were later charged with murder of the veterans. They were convicted and sentenced to twenty-five to forty years in prison. No one was ever charged with the murder of Everest.

Thurlby's cartoon illustrates the response of Governor Louis F. Hart to the labor violence. Hart urged state officials to wipe out all seditious activity. The printing plants of the *Union Record*, which many thought was the voice of Bolshevism, were seized by authorities, and efforts were made to deport all Wobblies. The only organization that placed blame for the violence on the City of Centralia was the Seattle Labor Council.

1920–1929

The Census Race

May 21, 1920
Ed "Tige" Reynolds
Tacoma Daily Ledger

At the beginning of 1920 Washington citizens anxiously awaited the results of the Census Bureau's population count. A big increase in population would promise economic growth, whereas a decrease would forebode doom and gloom for an area.

When the census figures were released in May Tacomans received them with mixed feelings. While the percentage gain for Tacoma was almost sixteen percent, Tacomans were disappointed that the rate of growth was slower than in the preceding decade and the city had not topped the 100,000 mark. They were even more disappointed that their city remained third in population behind Spokane. Tacomans, however, did find consolation in their figures when they learned that the number one city, Seattle, had shown very little growth, and the number two city, Spokane, had actually lost population.

Washington's Fairest Daughter Greets the President

July 27, 1923
Tom Thurlby
Seattle Daily Times

Predicting statehood for Alaska in the 1920s, President Warren G. Harding was greeted by throngs of Washingtonians as he and Mrs. Harding began their one-day visit to Seattle on July 27, 1923. This cartoon by Tom Thurlby shows the maiden Seattle greeting the President with the pomp accorded to national leaders.

The Hardings spent the day being surrounded by school children at Woodland and Volunteer Parks, prompting the *Seattle Daily Times* to ask the President to remember Seattle by its young people and their energy. A sentimental note was added to the president's visit when a contingent of old neighbors from Marion, Ohio, the President's hometown, bade the Hardings farewell at Union Station.

Unfortunately, Seattle was the last city the President would enjoy. Harding continued to weaken from the ptomaine poisoning he contracted while traveling down from Alaska, and he died the following week in San Francisco.

Two Reasons Why Crime Increases!

January 17, 1924
Sam Armstrong
Tacoma News Tribune

The Loose End of the System

December 23, 1924
Sam Armstrong
Tacoma News Tribune

Does it seem like "the more things change, the more things stay the same"? Cartoonist Sam Armstrong's comments on the coddling of criminals were drawn for the *Tacoma News Tribune* in 1924 and identifies a problem that persists today.

The cartoonist's specific complaint was the policy of Gov. Louis Hart, who paroled many criminals. The year before this cartoon was drawn, a man who was convicted of murder and mutilation served only a few months of his life sentence. Hart's rationale was that the murderer was an immigrant, and the governor wanted to deport the prisoner so he could serve his sentence in his native land. Over a two-year period Hart granted 110 executive paroles for all types of crimes.

At the Child Labor Hearing

January 20, 1925
Sam Armstrong
Tacoma News Tribune

The Only Animal That Exploits Its Young

January 26, 1925
Unknown
Seattle Post-Intelligencer

In the early 1900s nearly 1.5 million children under sixteen years of age—many under age ten—worked in America's factories and mines. They worked in despicable conditions, ten to thirteen hours a day, earning as little as sixty cents per day. In 1916 Congress passed the Child Labor Act which limited working hours and made illegal the interstate shipment of goods made by children. The United States Supreme Court, however, declared that law unconstitutional.

In 1924 Congress submitted to the states a proposed Twentieth Amendment to the Constitution—the Child Labor Amendment — which gave Congress the authority to legislate labor conditions for all children under eighteen. Governor Hartley claimed the amendment would "nationalize" the youth and ruin the family. The Washington state legislature considered the amendment in January, 1925, and after heated debate, Washington became the thirteenth and decisive state to reject ratification. Armstrong's cartoon was one of a series drawn about the legislature and this issue.

Look Out Below!

November 2, 1924

Tom Thurlby

Seattle Daily Times

The Ku Klux Klan reached its apex as an influential force in this country's politics during the 1920s when its membership numbered nearly four million nationwide. The Klan's attempt to inject its hatred into the social fabric of Washington caused outrage. *Seattle Daily Times* editor, C. B. Blethen, on July 12, 1923 sent a jolting message to the sheeted society:

"The Ku Klux Klan is the most dangerous thing that has ever come into American life. Washington wants none of it. . . . Americans wish to live in peace, and they intend to choose their own neighbors. . . . Any attempt on the part of the Ku Klux Klan to move in . . . will be considered and treated as an invasion of our country and a violation of our homes."

In November 1924 the Klan backed Initiative 49 which would have eliminated private and parochial schools and forced more than 18,000 children into public schools. On election day the voters handed the Klan a decisive defeat.

Where the Trouble Lies!

January 7, 1925
Sam Armstrong
Tacoma News Tribune

It was in the mid twenties that cartoonists began their war against reckless driving. In 1925 the New Year was greeted with the alarming statistic that nationwide there had been twenty-two thousand auto-related fatalities the previous year. Fatalities in Washington alone jumped twelve percent from 1923 to 1924, and judging from this cartoon by Armstrong, accidents were not the result of lady drivers. The cartoonist's message then would become universal: "Get the drunk and speeding driver off the road."

Time to Renew the Forests

November 20, 1924

Tom Thurlby

Seattle Daily Times

Although the global implications of deforestation were not well understood in 1924, citizens of Washington were concerned about the region's diminishing timber supply. In November the state held its fourth annual forestry conference.

Two key issues were discussed at the conference. One was how best to set up a reforestation program, the second was how to change the forest tax law so that private owners would have an incentive to reforest their land.

Just to Get Even With Teacher!

January 13, 1925
Sam Armstrong
Tacoma News Tribune

The depression for farmers in eastern Washington had started in 1924 because of drought. The nineteenth session of the legislature passed a $400,000 "seed wheat" bill to aid them. Also in 1924 Roland H. Hartley, a Republican, was elected governor. From the beginning of his two terms in office, Hartley was at odds with the legislature. Hartley vetoed the wheat bill because he felt it to be a costly boondoggle; and the legislature was outraged because the economy depended on the farm community. The House overrode Hartley's veto comfortably, but surprisingly, the Senate sustained it by one vote. Cartoonist Sam Armstrong depicts the depth of emotion over the issue. The fight was not to be Hartley's last, nor would it represent an end to attacks on him by the cartooning community.

The Target

October 5, 1926

Tom Thurlby

Seattle Daily Times

Self-government

October 8, 1926

Tom Thurlbly

Seattle Daily Times

In 1926 the University of Washington faced one of its gravest crises. It was the year the University almost died. The University had begun to achieve national recognition, and that year a record 6,500 students enrolled. But also that year Roland Hartley had faced a stormy session with the Legislature, and consistent with his conservative fiscal policy, made severe cuts in UW appropriations. The university president of eleven years, Henry Suzzallo, was publicly outraged at the treatment given public education.

On October 4, 1926 Dr. Suzzallo was called into the regents' board room and was asked to resign. He refused, and the regents, under the supervision of Governor Hartley, fired him. The reason given for Suzzallo's dismissal was that politics had become too dominant an influence in the affairs of the university president. Interestingly, Hartley was a Republican and Suzzallo had been very influential in state politics during the administration of Governor Lister—a Democrat. What resulted from that board meeting was the most vindictive cartoon campaign against any governor in Washington's history. For weeks, sometimes twice daily, Thurlby's cartoons led a recall fight against Hartley.

The press did not mince words either. Hartley was called "pitiful," "despicable," "bigoted," "childish," and a "windy demagogue." The recall effort against Hartley was the only time a Washington governor has faced one. After the dust had settled, the recall effort failed. Hartley did decide, however, to increase funding for education the next year, and in his moderation was reelected.

An Amazing Revelation!

February 1, 1926

Sam Armstrong

Tacoma News Tribune

In this cartoon Sam Armstrong shows the symbol of Washington state bewildered by news of corruption and a trial concerning Prohibition. And that's pretty much how average citizens felt about the onslaught of crime and evil during the days of the "noble experiment." A Seattle police officer, Roy Olmstead, decided to work both ends for profit when the Roaring Twenties dawned, but he was caught bootlegging, fined $500, and dismissed from the force. This just freed him to operate on a grander scale, and soon he was wholesaling illegal liquor, importing from Scotland, controlling Puget Sound as a rumrunner's haven, and grossing $200,000 a month. In 1924 he was arrested, but he posted bond and continued in "business." When his case came to trial he argued that he had been prosecuted on the basis of illegal wiretaps. Nevertheless he was convicted, with the Supreme Court upholding the verdict. In 1935 President Franklin Roosevelt pardoned the fallen police-officer-turned-bootlegger.

The Passing of the Old Days!

March 10, 1926
Sam Armstrong
Tacoma News Tribune

In the mayoral race of 1926 Tacoma citizens closed the book on the past and looked to the future. They had previously elected A. V. Fawcett as mayor four times, although never for consecutive terms. His first term began in 1896. This time, Fawcett was running for reelection on a record opposed to public libraries, a health department, and a modern transportation system. As cartoonist Sam Armstrong saw it, Fawcett no longer had anything positive to say about anything concerning the city he ran. Fawcett was defeated by M. G. Tennent, who talked about Tacoma's potential to voters and promised that Tacoma would attract more business and industry. Tennent was eventually elected to a second term.

Awaiting Our Bidding!

March 16, 1926
Sam Armstrong
Tacoma News Tribune

In the first two decades of Washington state history, Tacoma often found itself in the shadow of its northern neighbor, Seattle. In March 1926 one project lifted the spirits of Tacomans and marked a new era for this important port city—Cushman Dam. The dam and lake behind it were advertised as a scenic beauty site and, although man-made, was compared with the natural wonders of the Northwest. The first unit delivered 50,000 horsepower, the second unit 140,000 horsepower.

In April President Calvin Coolidge officially started operations at Cushman Dam by pressing a telegraph key carried to him by Lincoln High School student James Mosolf.

His Gay Bachelor Days Seem Over

March 22, 1926
Sam Armstrong
Tacoma News Tribune

Women continually played a role in the shaping of Washington. In March 1926 Bertha Knight Landes, a prohibitionist, became the first woman elected mayor of a major American city. As mayor of Seattle, Landes came into office in Seattle with impressive credentials. She was president of the Seattle Federation of Women's Clubs, and in 1921 organized the Women's Exhibit for Washington Manufacturers. That same year she was appointed to the mayor's commission on unemployment. She successfully ran for city council, was made council president, and was reelected to that position in 1924.

Landes defeated incumbent mayor Edwin J. Brown. While mayor, she brought about stricter law enforcement in the city, helped develop park programs, improved traffic safety, and supported appointments based on merit.

Homage At the Maple Court of King Basketball

March 14, 1929

Stuart Pratt

Seattle Post-Intelligencer

Every March Washington state goes nuts over the prep basketball championship, and this cartoon by Stuart Pratt is a great tribute to that event. The hoop tournament began in 1923 and for six years eastern Washington was king. The powers back then were not Redmond, Mercer Island, or Garfield. Walla Walla won the championship in 1923 and 1924, Yakima in 1925, Lewis and Clark in 1926, and North Central of Spokane in 1928. In 1927 Bothell became the first western school to capture the crown.

The final four in 1929 were North Central, Olympia, Mount Vernon, and Prosser, and the tournament was played at the University of Washington. There were no "run and gun" teams back then, and the emphasis was on defense. Coach "Chick" Rockey's Olympia team defeated North Central in the finals 26 to 17.

1930–1939

This Is Not the American Standard of Living, This Is!

February 6, 1931
Winsor McCay
Seattle Post-Intelligencer

This Too Will Pass

February 25, 1931
Winsor McCay
Seattle Post-Intelligencer

Over Production

September 16, 1931
T. Brown
Spokesman-Review

During the depression there were bankers who felt that the economy could best be helped by lowering public consumption levels to that of low production levels, thus achieving economic equilibrium. These "negative" thinking bankers did not consider raising production levels to meet the public demand, or increasing jobs and raising wages to increase demand and then production. In the 1930s cartoonists, as shown by this syndicated Winsor McCay cartoon, did what they could to reflect a more positive attitude of what the standard of living in America should be.

In February 1931 Washingtonians were turning to every source of strength to help pull themselves out of the Great Depression. The *Seattle Post-Intelligencer* ran this cartoon of Abraham Lincoln hoping to produce faith and inspiration for the future.

While people tried to hope for better times in 1931, faith was not always easy to maintain. There were all sorts of proposals made that often went beyond belief. One leader proposed a two-year moratorium on babies as an aid to the unemployed. The government proposed to set aside one-half million dollars to enable scientists to work on the problem. As this syndicated cartoon indicates, that proposal did not generate wide popular support.

Wings of the Morning, Noon and Night

April 3, 1931

Chopin

Seattle Post-Intelligencer

On April 1, 1931 the first coast-to-coast air service aboard a Boeing plane was illustrated and nationally syndicated. The thirty-two hour flight from Seattle's Boeing Field to New York had turned the country's major cities into suburbs of one another, and cartoonist Chopin captured that magic moment for the entire country.

That first continental service was one of the dreams of William Boeing whose company was born in July, 1916 as the Pacific Aero Products Company. Boeing soon became a household name in the aviation industry.

You've Gotta Hand It To Sam!

February 5, 1931

Fredrick Opper

Seattle Post-Intelligencer

They Wonder, We Do Not

April 19, 1931

Winsor McCay

Seattle Post-Intelligencer

Like the First World War, the Great Depression was not expected to last as long as it did. Knowing about the United States government's $5 billion in gold reserves, our European allies were beginning to question our economy's stagnation and wondering why the depression was stretching into 1931.

In early 1931, the *Seattle Post-Intelligencer* ran two cartoons by syndicated cartoonists which attempted to explain Washington state's and the whole country's dilemma—prohibition, bootlegging crime, and Uncle Sam's inaction. Eventually Congress, too, recognized what was sucking the life blood out of the country's recovery. In December 1933 the states ratified the Twenty-first Amendment to the United States Constitution, repealing the well-intentioned prohibition amendment. In January 1934 Washington state passed its Liquor Control Act and in March of that year the first state liquor store opened. It wasn't until March 1949, however, that people in the state could buy liquor by the drink.

And It Lives Up to the Promise

May 4, 1938

Dave McKay

Seattle Post-Intelligencer

At the end of the 1930s the misery index in Washington had declined enough so that newspapers turned to attracting people to the Northwest because of its recreation opportunities. Editorial cartoons frequently became advertisements for businesses and families who were seeking adventure outside their home states. These cartoons are representative of McKay's exuberant style. His drawings were executed in the style of the popular Dorman H. Smith, whose large drawings were populated with moving figures, crowded scenes, and labels galore during years of national syndication through the Newspaper Enterprise Association and the Hearst press. In the McKay cartoon, note that even the fishing scene in the background is animated.

The Horse-and-Buggy Days

May 25, 1938
Fred Marshall
Seattle Post-Intelligencer

A desire for the bygone days of the horse and buggy was not strong enough to keep construction on the Mercer Island Bridge from starting in December 1938. Prior to construction of the bridge, the Black Ball Line had two ferry runs in the area: the Lincoln run, which operated to and from Bellevue and downtown Seattle, and the Medina/Mercer Island run. The bridge set a high standard for the way public works projects were paid for—by revenue bonds, nineteen years ahead of time. It was named for its coordinator and the first director of state highway engineers, Lacey V. Murrow.

The Growing Giant

October 2, 1937

Dave McKay

Seattle Post-Intelligencer

Working Orders!

March 20, 1939

Fred Marshall

Seattle Post-Intelligencer

"Cast your eyes upon the biggest thing yet built by human hands.
On the King Columbia River, it's the Big Grand Coulee Dam."

These words of Woody Guthrie, written in 1941, were commissioned by the Bonneville Power Administration (BPA). In fact, the BPA made quite a deal with Guthrie to advertise the Grand Coulee, paying him only $266 for more than twenty songs, including "Roll On, Columbia."

Washingtonians have long noted the need for irrigation in eastern Washington, and as far back as Theodore Roosevelt's administration the federal government had considered supporting such a massive project. When the Depression hit, plans were revived for damming the Columbia River, not only to enrich central and eastern lands but also to provide jobs to construction workers. Seven thousand such workers toiled to turn 1.2 million acres into lush farmland via the Grand Coulee Dam, which was dedicated by Pres. Franklin Roosevelt in October 1937.

The visual shorthand in Dave McKay's cartoon has significance here: the electric bolts emanating from the giant's muscles suggest the very real hydroelectric promise of the Grand Coulee Dam. Grand Coulee would be dubbed "the eighth wonder of the world."

Wanted—a Guide

May 23, 1938
Fred Marshall
Seattle Post-Intelligencer

The fight was hard and long to establish one thousand square miles of land as a national park on the Olympic Peninsula. Cartoonist Fred Marshall of the *Seattle Post-Intelligencer* suggests confusion and shows "opposition" and "inaction" as culprits, but he failed to depict the real role played by timber interests in blocking the plan. The frightened plan of the drawing eventually found its way, thanks in large part to the efforts of U.S. Rep. Monrad C. Wallgren, who introduced enabling legislation in several sessions of Congress before winning the day on June 29, 1938. Today the Olympic remains one of the most spectacular national parks in the United States.

1940–1949

Johnny Doesn't Need a Gun

February 1, 1940

Walt Partymiller

Washington New Dealer

This cartoon was drawn for a notable voice of liberalism in the Pacific Northwest, the *Washington New Dealer*, later the *New World*. During the ravages of the depression Franklin Roosevelt's subtle shifts towards war dismayed those who sought a permanent role for the federal government in jobs and welfare programs. Ultimately, of course, the nation was forced to face wartime requirements, and Washington was to become (ironically, in view of this cartoon's prognosis) the major defense contractor among the states.

Woman Driver!

January 15, 1940
Irwin Caplan
The Seattle Star

Although sexually biased, this cartoon in 1940 served as an effective advertisement for the University of Washington's flying program. The University selected four girls and thirty-six boys to be trained by the government in a national air defense program. Alice Hitchkiss was the first to successfully solo after the government training.

It'o Happoning In Olympia

February 6, 1941

Ben Yomen

Washington New Dealer

Labor strife was a factor in the state's life in the 1930s and early 1940s, when both the Great Depression and the onset of the Second World War made the right to strike a matter of vital debate. The antistrike law referred to in this cartoon was SB 99 or the "Model Anti-Sabotage" law. It passed the Senate, but died in a House committee.

Although this cartoon was signed "Ben Yomen," it was actually drawn by the noted political cartoonist William Gropper. A respected printmaker and lithographer, Gropper was also an effective political cartoonist whose work graced a range of publications from the socialist *Masses* in the new century's second decade to the communist *Liberator* in the 1920s to the trendy *Vanity Fair* in the 1930s. His reputation was such that Washington papers would import his work, and the social and political issues in Washington were such that Gropper's cartoon would offer relevant commentary.

Labor Working with Uncle Sam

October 6, 1941
Fred Marshall
Seattle Post-Intelligencer

What makes this Fred Marshall cartoon so powerful is that the cartoon itself is the headline. Like cartoons at the beginning of the century, this front page cartoon shaped the news. In October 1941 the American Federation of Labor held its convention in Seattle and made decisions affecting its five million membership. The AFL convention endorsed war aid to the Soviet Union while attacking communism. It also adopted resolutions to eliminate racketeers and a program to relieve unemployment.

The two major speakers at the convention were AFL President William Green and Ruth Taylor, leader of the labor press. Green promised the British labor movement that American labor would lay down its life to defend the principles of freedom; Taylor called upon all delegates to remain firm in their convictions for better working conditions and labor unity. Nothing that week could speak stronger, however, for labor's contribution to America than this Marshall cartoon.

Their Fine Feathered Friends

October 27, 1941

Fred Marshall

Seattle Post-Intelligencer

The State of Washington was involved in the Second World War long before
Congress declared war. A good example was the Greater Seattle Defense Chest
drive. Its symbol was a red feather in one's cap, given in exchange for
donations. The chairman was R. Kline Hillman whose "army" of eight
thousand workers raised close to a million dollars. During drives, as this
cartoon suggests, virtually everyone on Seattle's streets could be seen with a
feather. The Defense Chest drive was joined with the Community Chest to
include the needs of local service organizations and the United China Relief
Fund. In 1941 China had long been invaded by Japan. "A thing like this drive
is a test of our ability to keep the American way of doing things," Hillman said.
The Defense and Community Chest later became the United Way.

Making It Tough to Fill

May 29, 1942
Unknown
Seattle Star

Food for our soldiers made Washington the focus of national attention in the spring of 1942. Secretary of the Interior Harold L. Ickes had issued an order that recognized Alaskan Indians' first rights to Pacific salmon. At the time fisheries was the second largest industry in Washington state, and Ickes's decision took away the 1942 salmon pack which many citizens depended on for employment and which the army depended on as food for the troops.

Ickes's decree caused an outburst of anger by cartoonists, the press, and the state's politicians. They felt the enemy was being comforted and asked for a moratorium on native American fishing until the 1942 salmon season was completed. U.S. Sen. Monrad C. Wallgren of Everett introduced a bill in Congress that called for allocation of fishing sites between Indian and non-Indian fishermen. His bill died in committee and was not reintroduced in the next session.

And We'll Work the Harder!

June 9, 1942

Fred Marshall

Seattle Post-Intelligencer

Through the years cartoonists have represented the State of Washington in many forms—usually as a figure resembling George himself, sometimes as a matronly protectress, occasionally as a noble Columbia-type, right off images on medallions and friezes. But to cartoonist Fred Marshall, Washington should *look* like Washington, so he affixed a face and stuck legs on an outline of the Evergreen State. No matter, his pictorialization was as spirited as any cartoonist's, as were his themes.

Of all of Washington's many cartoonists through one hundred years, Marshall was one of the state's biggest boosters. This cartoon, drawn in the darkest days of the Second World War, served as a promotional poster for vacationing in Washington.

Step Aside, Oaf

Date Unknown
Sam Groff
Seattle Times

Washingtonians love baseball, and the Seattle Rainiers brought pride to the diamond in the early forties and late fifties. This cartoon by Sam Groff was one of many that Groff drew for one Rainiers' season. The Rainiers had acquired William Franklin Skiff as their new manager for the 1941 season after the death of Jack Lelivelt. "Bill" Skiff and Emil Sick's Rainiers won the pennant and President's Cup (playoffs) in 1941.

Often featured in Groff's 1942 cartoons would be Elmer d'Rainier chasing or cruising around with Beulah—the league lead or championship. Groff's style was fun and vaudevillian, and other teams in the league could often be seen performing pratfalls because of the talented Rainiers. In 1942 the Rainiers defeated the Los Angeles Angels for the President's Cup.

Equal Pay for Equal Work

March 11, 1943

Dave Mero

Washington New Dealer

Equal rights for women was the state's official labor policy during the Second World War. Dave Mero commented in the *New Dealer* on the work and pay of women who took men's work as soldiers went off to war. In 1943 HB 14—the "Comparable Worth" legislation—passed overwhelmingly and was signed by Governor Langlie. This wartime statute was evidently forgotten in recent years when similar legislation was proposed and hotly debated in the legislature and then the courts. Issues like equal pay for equal work and comparable worth remained the same through the years, but as the Mero cartoon illustrates, at one time Washingtonians were unified on the subject.

SAVE WASTE FATS—
They make BULLETS!

Out of the Frying Pan—Into the Firing Line!!

March 25, 1943
Alston
New World

Washington's *New World* spurred readers to assist the war effort and forcefully advocated positions like opening a Second Front. But on the home front its cartoons (like this drawing by Alston) urged readers to engage in cottage-industry war efforts promoted by the war department. Saving fats was one such activity (it was claimed that a pound of fat helped produce a half pound of dynamite or four 37-mm. antiaircraft shells). Other activities included saving tin foil and scrap paper and planting "victory gardens."

Cleaning House

April 30, 1942
Walt Partymiller
Washington New Dealer

Restricted Education

January 29, 1948
Cartoonist Unknown
New World

These cartoons address the issue of prejudice in Washington state. At the time of their publication, the Supreme Court was dealing with the constitutionality of restrictive covenants, paving the way for the era of civil rights legislation. Covenants that forbade ownership of property because of race or religion once were common throughout Washington.

Although Walt Partymiller's cartoon shows the arm of the U.S. removing race discrimination, the policies of government agencies fostered unfair treatment of individuals in many areas. The second cartoon portrays the prejudice in higher education that existed at this time in Washington state. Most frequently it was directed against Japanese-Americans. During the war these citizens were not only barred from classrooms, but were interned in camps in Idaho, Arizona, and California.

"You'll have to wait, son, till we check on your race and religion!"

Un-American Committee

February 5, 1948

Walt Partymiller

New World

As the Cold War between the United States and the Soviet Union became more intense, fear of communism spread throughout Washington. Even before Joseph McCarthy cast his shadow across this country, state Sen. Albert Canwell chaired an un-American committee which eventually led to the dismissal of three University of Washington faculty members. The Canwell investigation ended in July 1948 and was endorsed by many papers across Washington. One paper, however, that denounced Canwellism and his "guilt by association" inquiry was the *New World*. In this cartoon Walt Partymiller reflects not only the belief of the *New World* but the reaction of many Americans to these "investigative" committees.

Ban the Ban Against Free Speech

March 2, 1948
Wing Luke
The University of Washington Daily

Wing Luke drew this cartoon as a student when the University of Washington banned on-campus appearances of all political speakers. In response the student body considered three policies: (1) keeping the ban, (2) permitting speakers except for "avowed" communists, and (3) permitting all political speakers. Under the leadership of then student body vice-president Brock Adams, the students voted to lift the ban on *all* speakers. This vote was sustained by the highest student organization, the Control Board; however, the University administration maintained the right to veto any speaker.

Bring a Brick—For Better Health!

October 1, 1949

Cartoonist Unknown

Pacific Northwest Cooperator

An effective cartoon can even help change the medical profession. This cartoon was successful in enlisting Group Health Cooperative members to buy bonds for a new medical and dental clinic.

The Group Health Cooperative opened its doors to members at Saint Luke's hospital in Seattle on January 1, 1947. Its goal was to enlist members who would own part of the co-op and vote on its policies. Group Health, however, was considered a radical idea by the established medical profession and many Group Health doctors found themselves blacklisted from other hospitals. New doctors coming into Group Health could not get licenses. Seattle attorney Jack Cluck sued the medical establishment on behalf of Group Health doctors and its members. Group Health lost the trial in 1948 but won when the case was appealed to the Washington State Supreme Court. After forty years Group Health continues to do its own financing and has become the largest member-owned health care center in the country.

1950–1959

After This Apple's Taken Care of—

July 14, 1950
Shaw McCutcheon
Spokesman-Review

Washington state's apples are popular not only for their taste but also for their size. The apple featured in this Shaw McCutcheon cartoon, however, was one apple too big to be carried by the taxpayers—a burden created by welfare payments. In July 1950 the Legislature appropriated more funds for welfare grants mandated by Initiative 172. More than $22 million was being requested by support groups and legislators from around the state. Although many citizens, including McCutcheon, believed Initiative 172 was flawed, the special session could not amend or abolish it.

In November 1950 voters approved Initiative 178, a law that sought to make welfare recipients more accountable for the support they received.

Possible Precautionary Measure

November 14, 1951
Shaw McCutcheon
Spokesman Review-Chronicle

Seattle may have been the birthday boy, but the guest of honor made the headlines. The Seattle Centennial Committee invited Gen. Douglas MacArthur to be the opening speaker in a year-long celebration of the city's history. Some people questioned the decision to give a forum to a man who had been fired from his command seven months earlier by Democratic Pres. Harry Truman. MacArthur did not disappoint these people as he used the Seattle celebration as a soapbox for a blistering attack on the Democratic administration. He spoke of a "creeping sabotage of freedom by the federal government" that threatened to put an "iron curtain" over America and wreck its living standards.

Blanket Primary System

February 8, 1953

Shaw McCutcheon

Spokesman-Review

Every state but two has an open or closed primary voting system. In February 1935 the State of Washington (and later Alaska), through an initiative to the legislature, adopted the blanket primary. To the chagrin of both major parties, Washington voters in a primary election are able to demonstrate their political independence by voting for any candidate listed on the ballot regardless of the voter's party affiliation.

The efforts for this initiative began when the Washington State Grange, a nonpartisan organization, wanted to strengthen its influence in the state. It felt that the best way to accomplish this was by voting for the most qualified people instead of one party.

Showing How to Cut It Down

February 17, 1954
Shaw McCutcheon
Spokesman-Review

In November 1953 three-term governor Arthur B. Langlie declared a "campaign of war" against individuals whose traffic violations were responsible for death and injury. The national traffic fatality toll had risen above thirty-eight thousand in 1953, and statewide fatalities resulted not only in the loss of innocent lives but also ran up a bill of more than $44 million. Langlie's campaign included "sneaker cars" driven by plain clothesmen, radar, and random spotters.

McCutcheon's cartoon gives the reader insight into the governor's character. Langlie was an accomplished athlete at the University of Washington, and in this cartoon his physical abilities are once again being tested as he successfully tops the traffic toll tree.

Draft McCarthy

May 13, 1954

Charlotte Groff

Bellevue American

Charlotte Groff followed in her father's footsteps by incorporating a reader's poem in her cartoons. Readers were encouraged to contribute a verse to the topic of the day. Many Americans became concerned when Sen. Joseph McCarthy publicly accused the State Department of being infiltrated by communists. McCarthyism began a whole new vocabulary for some as this cartoon illustrates. In fact, the word "McCarthyism" was first used by *Washington Post* cartoonist Herbert Block, who in 1950 showed the word crudely lettered on a barrel of mud resting precariously on a tower made up of pockets of mud.

Another Step Up the Fish Ladder

September 23, 1954
Shaw McCutcheon
Spokesman-Review

Under a hot September sun the Twenty-first Army Band from Fort Lewis played "Hail to the Chief" as thirty thousand northwesterners greeted Pres. Dwight D. Eisenhower at the dedication of McNary Dam. "I have the greatest sense of distinction and pride in the government's part in this project," Eisenhower said. With those words the president pushed a button that started McNary's fifth of fourteen generators. Washington state officials at the dedication included Governor Langlie and U.S. Sen. Henry M. Jackson.

McNary was not just another link in the chain of dams that made the Columbia River the most fully developed river in the country. McNary has a navigation lock, permitting river barges to run the Umatilla rapids and carry products up and down the Columbia; and fish ladders, enabling salmon to get to spawning beds. Although McCutcheon's salmon is smiling, the dam's construction also destroyed many ancient fishing and spawning grounds.

Disastrous for a Fellow's Dignity

November 26, 1955

Shaw McCutcheon

Spokesman-Review

The people of Stevens County overwhelming voted against power distribution by a Public Utility District (PUD) in November 1955. Ken Billington, executive secretary of Washington's PUD association, stated that he regretted to see citizens give up local ownership and the move towards lower rates. Kirsey M. Robinson, president of Washington Water Power, saw it another way. He felt the vote supported free enterprise power and that Stevens County families would not have to use oil lamps anymore. This public versus private power election received national attention. It was the first time since the PUD movement was authorized by the state legislature in 1907 that the people affected were able to vote and choose how they wanted their power serviced.

The Stevens County election helped establish the standard that power in Washington state would be both publicly and privately controlled.

Surely Something's in the Air

January 26, 1958
Alan Pratt
Seattle Times

This cartoon by Al Pratt illustrates the beginning of the state government's concern about air quality in Washington. The Health Department finally began to conclude what citizens already knew—that some places in the state had an odoriferous quality about them.

Although researching air pollution in Washington has been around for three decades now, it was only in 1986 under the Federal Emergency Planning and Right-to-Know law that the public finally obtained access to information concerning the toxic chemicals emitted by specific industries. The state Department of Ecology is now in charge of keeping pollution records. While industries are required by law to maintain records of chemicals released into the air, land, or water, most of the 328 toxins listed by the federal government are still not regulated by law.

Rescue Ladder

February 28, 1959
Shaw McCutcheon
Spokesman-Review

Thomas Jefferson said democracy can best be protected by the education of our youth. When there is a crisis in one, the other is threatened. This cartoon by Shaw McCutcheon has come back to haunt the Washington public. Public education, which consumes 44 percent of the state budget, is still in a financial squeeze. To meet the future demand for teachers 23 percent of students entering state colleges should be going into education; instead, only 7 percent are headed toward the classroom.

The idea that students can be rescued from this crisis by filling up a room and turning on the projector or, today, a VCR, is not farfetched. Many "professionals" have considered the idea. A question is posed by McCutcheon's cartoon: are tomorrow's students really stepping up a rescue ladder or stepping into a video-controlled environment?

Sacajawea, 1959

June 6, 1959
Shaw McCutcheon
Spokesman-Review

With a little help from cartoonist McCutcheon, Sacajawea finds herself leading another group of important citizens west—this time it is presidential hopefuls. The candidates McCutcheon specifically mentions are Democrats Stuart Symington, Hubert Humphrey, and John Kennedy. It was in this election that Washington was finally identified as an important "swing" state, never to be ignored again.

Kennedy's visit created the most press, of course. Accompanied by Jackie, Kennedy made a three-day tour of Washington, stopping in Seattle, Tacoma, and Yakima. While in Seattle, Kennedy asked voters to judge him on his abilities and not by his religion. He also blasted Jimmy Hoffa as a hoodlum. Although JFK charmed the public, the state's electoral votes still went to Richard Nixon in 1960.

Something To Sink Your Teeth Into

January 1, 1960

Bob McCausland

Seattle Post-Intelligencer

When the University of Washington Huskies earned the right to represent the Pacific Coast League (now the Pac-10) in the 1960 Rose Bowl, they knew that the Big Ten would be lining up some big bullies on the other side of scrimmage. Cartoonist McCausland's pregame drawings show how the Big Ten had "picked" its way to victory in twelve of thirteen previous meetings between the two leagues and how the Huskies hoped to get some roses of their own. On New Year's Day the Huskies took a solid bite out of the "neighbor kids" and brought respect back to the West Coast. The Dawgs scored six touchdowns and one field goal in defeating the Wisconsin Badgers 44–8. Husky halfback George Fleming and quarterback Bob Schloredt were selected the most valuable players. Husky coach Jim Owens was only thirty-two when this win snapped a bowl losing streak dating back to 1924.

1960–1969

Sneak Preview

April 21, 1962

Shaw McCutcheon

Spokesman-Review

A Lot Going On In There

April 19, 1962

Fred Marshall

Seattle Post-Intelligencer

The Century 21 exposition was Washington's Easter present to the rest of the world, and Fred Marshall's cartoon welcomed the world's fair to this state. Maybe one reason why Marshall's fair egg is so big and making so much noise is because the fair was seven years in preparation.

Symbolized by the Space Needle, Century 21 was the first world's fair in America in twenty years, and it was much more than just expectation. At noon on April 21 Pres. John F. Kennedy tapped a golden telegraph key in Palm Beach. It was the same key used by Pres. William Howard Taft to begin the Alaska-Yukon-Pacific Exposition in Seattle in 1909. This time, however, the golden key started a space antenna in Andover, Maryland, which began a search into space for a star signal nearing the planet. American Telephone & Telegraph Co. relayed the star signal to Seattle which began the fair. The twist in all of this is that a world's fair about "tomorrow" began with a star signal 10,000 years old.

Showing No Signs of Stopping

June 1, 1965

Shaw McCutcheon

Spokesman-Review

Citizens of Washington state delight in the fact that they are among the few Americans who do not have to pay a state income tax. Only seven other states do not levy such taxes. In June 1965 cartoonist McCutcheon decided to show the flip-side of the issue—if citizens do not pay one way, they will pay another. Now at 6.5 percent plus local levies, Washington has one of the highest sales taxes in the country, and this tax comprises 47 percent of total state tax revenue. Shaw McCutcheon demonstrated that he knew more than the political pundits when he titled this cartoon.

Yakima's Bitter Harvest

September 15, 1967
Walt Crowley
Helix

Walt Crowley's *Helix* showed Washingtonians the unspeakable in this powerful cartoon. During the 1960s the government, as represented here by the eagle, was blind to the need of the farm workers. While growers bragged about the profits from their crops, the migrant family suffered from poor wages and horrific living conditions. There was no union representation back then, but the farm worker had a strong advocate in cartoonist Crowley.

Selective Service

April 7, 1967

Steve McKinstry

Ingraham High School *Cascade*

As its legislative sunset in June 1967 approached, lawmakers and the public alike debated the merits of the nation's selective service system. The draft law was used increasingly to conscript young men for service in Vietnam, but students in college generally qualified for deferments. Some argued that the burdens of service fell unfairly on the poor and undereducated. When this cartoon was drawn the idea of choosing men by lottery was just a proposal.

Y'all Is Traders

June 11, 1967
Ray Collins
Seattle Post-Intelligencer

Washington families were greatly affected by the Vietnam War and the antiwar movement. Three hundred thousand Washington men and women went to Vietnam, and of the 580 who have their names etched in a black granite memorial, 58 are still missing in action. U.S. Sen. Henry M. Jackson supported the war, believing that our commitment to Vietnam would stop the spread of communism around the world. Others argued that Vietnam was fighting a civil war that was killing our nation's youth and draining our national resources and spirit.

Demonstrations were held throughout the state. A group known as the Seattle Seven was found guilty of destroying parts of a federal courthouse, and they were sentenced to prison. After American commitment escalated and Cambodia was bombed, ten thousand protest marchers blocked traffic on Interstate 5 for hours. Protesters also demonstrated on campus against the University of Washington's contracts with companies that made war materials. This Ray Collins cartoon evokes the antiwar movement at the UW during Lyndon Johnson's administration.

Can Seattle Come Out and Play Now?

February 13, 1968

Bob McCausland

Seattle Post-Intelligencer

I Guess This Means Good-bye

February 14, 1968

Alan Pratt

Seattle Times

Forward Thrust, a Seattle civic booster organization, was the brainchild of James Ellis, Franklin High School graduate and Seattle lawyer. The group's agenda promised to take Seattle and King County into the twenty-first century. Believing that the boom years at Boeing would loosen voter pocket books, Ellis and his Forward Thrust organizers put together a package calling for $385 million for rail transit, $121 million for parks, $78 million for arterial highways, $70 million for storm sewers in Seattle, $68 million for flood control, and $40 million for a domed stadium for major league sports.

Bob McCausland's cartoon shows how major league sports teams and advocates supported the domed stadium. Together the projects meant over a half-billion dollars in increased taxes. The voters cast their ballots in February 1968.

Cartoonist Al Pratt approved of the results, and he could not resist using a visual pun in this cartoon. The bond issues for parks, highways, sewer, and the stadium (now the King Dome) were approved. Pratt saw the results as the voter "thrusting" old Seattle "forward" over the cliff. On the other hand, the rail transit bonds were turned down. To Ellis and others this was a major setback for the future.

Wettest Year on Record

Winter 1968

Alan Pratt

Seattle Times

A cartoon book about Washington would be incomplete without a modern cartoon about the weather. In this drawing Al Pratt serves notice to all potential Washingtonians that the Washington coastal district, including cities on Puget Sound, is the least sunny area in the United States. And if newcomers want proof of the area's considerable cloudiness, all they need to do is ask natives to expose the webs between their toes.

The wettest year on record is still 1968. In that year, western Washington recorded 50.14 inches of rain, twelve inches above the mean average.

The SST

November 9, 1969

Irwin Caplan

Seattle Times

One of the biggest technological debates to face Washingtonians in the state's first century was the development of the Supersonic Transport (SST). The plane was controversial due to its tremendous cost: from 1962 to 1971 the federal government invested $1.3 billion in development alone. National pride was at stake because four other countries also were vying to produce the world's first commercially viable SST. Washington state became more interested in the outcome of the gamble after Boeing was chosen in 1966 to build the American SST.

Although successful completion of the SST meant prestige for the United States, more jobs for Boeing, and a potential for improvements in the U.S. balance of payments, environmental problems and poor economics ultimately scuttled the plane.

Washington's economy was hurt by that decision. Britain continued its program and successfully "hatched" the Concord. As for the United States, the most that can be said for its $1.3 billion investment was that it laid an egg.

Rolling out the Carpet

April 10, 1969
Alan Pratt
Seattle Times

The Seattle Pilots walked into Washington on a red carpet in 1969, as one of four teams formed during baseball's second expansion. The state finally had a major league ball club, and the fans were ready to go wild. On opening day U.S. Sen. Warren Magnuson threw out the first pitch and the Pilots beat the California Angels 4-3. The Pilots were having an exciting first season up to the All-Star game, but then injuries escorted the Pilots toward the cellar. In one stretch the team lost twenty-one of twenty-four games, and the Pilots lost every home game in August. As the team's fortunes dwindled, player Jim Bouton continued to keep the baseball diary he would later promote into a scandalous best seller—*Ball Four*. On October 2 the Pilots' season ended with a 3-1 loss to the Oakland Athletics, and the Pilots finished dead last. While the end of the 1960s rolled out the carpet for the pilots, the 1970s pulled the rug out from under them.

1970–1979

Shipwrecked

February 1970

Bob McCausland

Seattle Post-Intelligencer

While Al Pratt's earlier cartoon of the Seattle Pilots was a hopeful first chapter to the team's history, this poignant Bob McCausland cartoon is the closing chapter of the financially shipwrecked team. In January 1970 the Bank of California called in its $3.5 million loan made to the Pilots' owners. Pilot president and former Rainier pitcher Dewey Soriano struggled to revitalize the team's financial standing. Businessman Fred Danz recommended a three-year advance ticket sale to prove to the principal owner, William Daley, that the community was behind the Pilots. One million dollars was even raised to remodel Sick Stadium. As Bud Selig watched the wounded Seattle ball club from Milwaukee and waited to move in for the kill, Gov. Dan Evans and Mayor Wes Uhlman got behind Danz's efforts. Although the ticket sale was successful, local banks failed to get behind the organization. A week before the Pilots were to begin their second season, a bankruptcy court approved the sale of the Pilots to Selig. Overnight the Seattle Pilots became the Milwaukee Brewers.

Report From the Front

March 15, 1970

Alan Pratt

Seattle Times

The "war" for Fort Lawton is almost as old as the State of Washington. In this one cartoon Al Pratt documents the final battle. In 1900 a new Army post was established on one thousand acres of Magnolia Bluff in Seattle and named Fort Lawton after Maj. Gen. Henry Ware Lawton. In January 1917 the Army established another military base in the area—Fort Lewis, and Seattle began making efforts to have Fort Lawton converted into a park.

Seattle had opportunities to purchase the fort grounds in the 1930s and again in the 1960s, when the federal government announced that the fort site would be declared surplus. The final battle was fought in 1970, and Al Pratt's cartoon does not miss anything. Everyone wanted a piece of the action—from real estate developers to bird watchers to native Americans, who occupied the fort to assert their claim to the land.

In October 1970 the Washington congressional delegation helped pass a bill permitting cities to acquire surplus federal lands at no cost for park and recreation purposes, and Discovery Park became a reality. The park and its Indian Cultural Center are now enjoyed by thousands of people every year.

Hijack Job

July 7, 1970

Shaw McCutcheon

Spokesman-Review

The Biggest and Tallest

Circa 1973

Bob McCausland

Seattle Post-Intelligencer

In the late 1950s the Boeing Company employed about every other manufacturing worker in King County—boom years for Boeing, Seattle, and Washington. The boom went bust, however, in 1970, and Shaw McCutcheon's cartoon shows the feelings of many citizens as Boeing laid off nearly two-thirds of its work force.

There were two major reasons for the 1970–71 recession. First, the demand for Boeing 747s fell far short of expectations, and second, the SST on which Boeing depended was dropped by Congress in 1971. Seattle residents joked about their city becoming a ghost town, and the last person to leave was asked to turn off the lights.

In late 1973 cartoonist Bob McCausland showed how Boeing's rebounding employment levels compared to large public employers in Washington and Puget Sound. Alongside William Boeing is King County Executive John Spellman, Seattle Mayor Wes Uhlman, and, of course, Pres. Richard Nixon. This is one of the few cartoons that depicts Gov. Dan Evans with a beard. Evans sprouted his beard during a summer vacation on Orcas Island, but showed up for his "State of the State" address the following January with a clean chin.

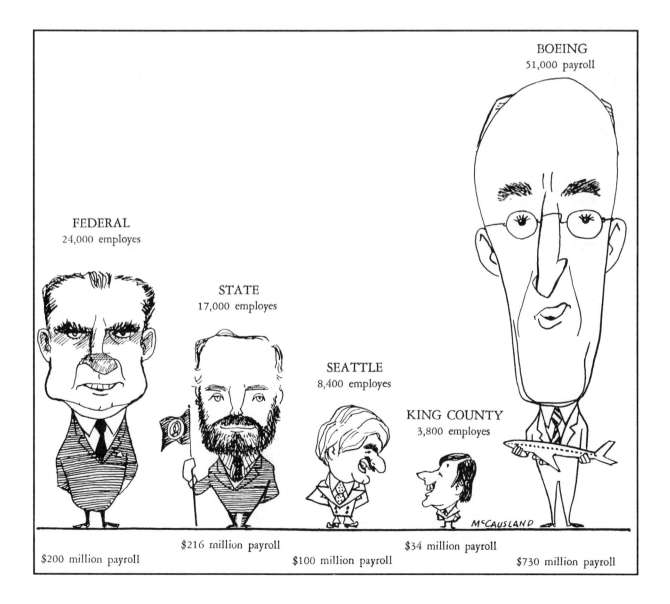

BOEING
51,000 payroll

FEDERAL
24,000 employes

STATE
17,000 employes

SEATTLE
8,400 employes

KING COUNTY
3,800 employes

McCAUSLAND

$216 million payroll

$200 million payroll

$100 million payroll

$34 million payroll

$730 million payroll

Tax Revision

October 28, 1973

Bob McCausland

Seattle Post-Intelligencer

As well as any presidential debate, these two Bob McCausland cartoons show how voters look at issues in differesnt ways. In this case the issue is the 1973 proposed state income tax. HJR 37 was a proposed amendment to the state constitution, and it was approved by two-thirds of both the House and the Senate and then submitted to the voters. The income tax would also have prohibited local levies for school operations. On election day the measure was overwhelmingly defeated.

Rest In Peace, Husky

November 26, 1973
Bob McCausland
Seattle Post-Intelligencer

Bob McCausland is well known for his cartoon series "Hairbreadth Husky." During the 1973 football season the Huskies were a hairbreadth away from total debacle until the last game, when they finally hit bottom. This cartoon serves as the season's obituary. The last game was the annual "Apple Cup" between the Cougars and the Huskies, and the Huskies were mangled 52-26. Coach Sweeney's Cougars scored record high points against the Dawgs, and Cougar quarterback Chris Rowland's four touchdown passes put him at fifteen TD passes for the season which tied Sonny Sixkiller's old record. The UW loss made the Husky Pac-8 season 0-7.

Till Death Do You Part

May 4, 1974

Shaw McCutcheon

Spokesman-Review

The Spirit of '74

May 5, 1974

Shaw McCutcheon

Spokesman-Review

For an area that has more than one hundred lakes within a day's drive, Spokane could not have chosen a more fitting name for Expo '74 than "Mankind and His Environment." The fair was first conceived to be only regional, but as promoter King Cole and the Spokane business community became more excited about its possibilities, it grew and grew until pavilions from all over the world were included. In financing the fair the City of Spokane bought bonds which were later paid for by local Business and Occupation taxes. Burlington Northern donated and traded land along the Spokane River so the city could use its wonderful natural environment as part of the fair site.

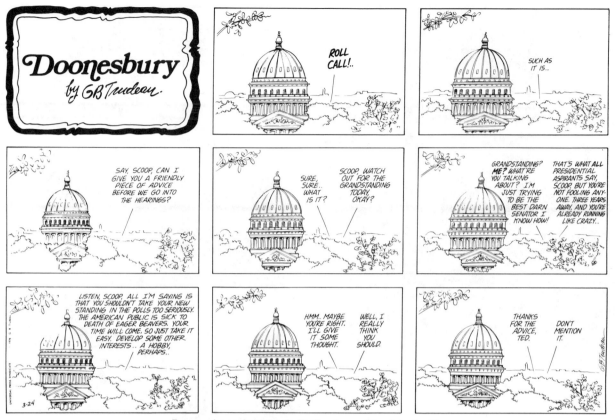

Doonesbury

March 24, 1974

Garry Trudeau

Universal Press Syndicate

Henry Jackson was Washington state's "favorite son," and his runs for the presidency in 1972 and 1976 were cartooned nationally. During these campaigns "Scoop" and fellow presidential candidate Teddy Kennedy frequently found themselves together in the same cartoon.

In the 1972 campaign Jackson took his delegates all the way to the divisive Democratic convention in Miami where George McGovern finally won the nomination. In 1976, after having won the New York and Massachusetts primaries, Jackson lost in Pennsylvania to Jimmy Carter. Contributions to Jackson's campaign started to dry up, and eventually he withdrew from the race and freed his delegates in the name of "unity."

© 1975 by Herblock in the Washington Post

Douglas

December 5, 1975

Paul Conrad

Los Angeles Times

American Mountain

December 5, 1975

Herbert Block

Washington Post

William O. Douglas was committed to the ideals of free thought and conservation of our natural resources. As a child Douglas moved to Yakima, and in the mountains that he grew to love, he built the physical strength to overcome the effects of polio. Following service on the Securities and Exchange Commission, Pres. Franklin D. Roosevelt appointed Douglas to the Supreme Court. Douglas retired in 1975 after a record-breaking thirty-six years on the high court.

While a justice Douglas returned to Washington state many times, sometimes to relax at Goose Prairie and other times to show his support for protection of the state's natural beauty. When he died in 1975 some of the great cartoonists from all over the country mourned his passing with images of the environment he worked to preserve.

Funny, We Hadn't Noticed

August 26, 1977
Shaw McCutcheon
Spokesman-Review

Washington state has a long tradition of leading the other states of the union with social legislation and reforms that were later adopted elsewhere. Cartoonist McCutcheon points out that during the national debate over the Equal Rights Amendment, a heated topic during much of the 1970s, Washington was already in the "ratified" column.

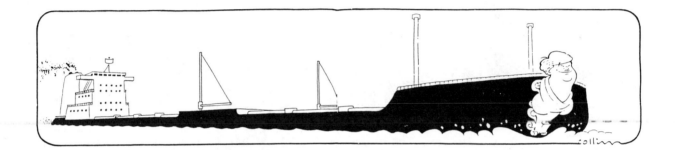

Dixy at the Helm

March 22, 1977

Ray Collins

Seattle Post-Intelligencer

A decade ago petroleum companies proposed that Washington state become a major transshipment point for Alaskan crude oil. Gov. Dixy Lee Ray agreed, and she vetoed a bill that would have mandated that any supertanker port be located outside of Puget Sound. She even stood on the helm of one supertanker as a symbolic affirmation of her belief in the safety of such vessels.

Cherry Point or Bust

October, 1977
David Horsey
Bellevue Daily Journal-American

U.S. Sen. Warren G. Magnuson, a fierce environmentalist, engineered one of the shrewdest legislative maneuvers in state history when he slipped an amendment into a federal law that prohibited supertankers from entering Puget Sound.

As one of the country's finest legislators and Washington's greatest advocates, Senator Magnuson always seemed bigger than life. In this cartoon David Horsey of the *Daily Journal-American* depicted Maggie as a powerful Neptune—and the public opinion behind his action helped vote Governor Ray out of office in the next election.

Cecil C. Addle

Circa 1977

Ray Collins

Seattle Post-Intelligencer

In 1975 Ray Collins of the *Seattle Post-Intelligencer* created a provincial comic strip that appeared on the Op-Ed page. The editorial strip featured Dipstick—a black saltwater duck and Cecil—just a regular, kind man, who represented the viewpoint of the minority and the so-called lunatic fringe. The strip always had a persecutor (someone from the outside), a victim (Cecil or Dipstick) and a rescuer (a log where victims went to contemplate). This cartoon strip evokes Gov. Dixy Lee Ray's support for an oil pipeline terminal in Puget Sound.

Ship of State

July 4, 1977
Bob McCausland
Seattle Post-Intelligencer

This cartoon of Washington's political powers was drawn by Bob McCausland during the 1977 legislative session. What makes the cartoon so fascinating is not only the caricatures but what has happened to everyone politically since 1977. In fact, if McCausland were to rename his ship today, he would probably call it the "Ship of *Fate*."

State Sen. August Mardesich was the powerful majority leader from Everett. He lost his leadership position to Gordon Walgren from Bremerton in December 1975 after Mardesich was accused and brought to trial for extortion and campaign violations. Mardesich was acquitted, but in 1978 he was defeated in a primary election.

Just as Walgren was hoisting his sails in the Senate, he was brought to trial in 1980 by an FBI sting operation. Walgren, along with Speaker of the House John Bagnariol, became a leading character in what came to be known as the Gamscam trial. Both legislators were convicted of trying to help mobsters control gambling in Washington.

Hubert Donohue of Columbia County was chairman of the Senate Ways and Means Committee in 1977. He left office in 1980. A. N. "Bud" Shinpoch was often called "the conscience of the legislature," but he, too, is gone. For fifteen years he was a representative and then senator from Renton. He retired in 1984. All shipwrecks have their sole survivor, and Seattle Rep. Helen Sommers is still anchored down in the Washington state legislature.

'OK, men, if we can't break up the oil giants, the least we can do is break up these big farm spreads.'

1902 Law

January 6, 1978
Shaw McCutcheon
Spokesman-Review

In 1978 Pres. Jimmy Carter and Secretary of the Interior Cecil Andrus began to enforce a 1902 law that excluded farms larger than 160 acres from receiving water from federal reclamation projects. The law also stated that farmers needed to live on or near the farm. Until Carter's administration the law was largely ignored in the West.

Nowhere was the protest against Carter's action as strong as along the Columbia River. Although some absentee landowners were taking advantage of the law, most farmers needed all of their land for economic survival. The U.S. District Court held that an Environmental Impact Statement must be completed on each farm before the farm was broken up. This, coupled with the severe protests, prompted the Carter administration to modify its enforcement policies.

Through the Hoop

Circa 1978

David Horsey

Bellevue Daily Journal-American

During Dixy Lee Ray's term in office, cartoonist David Horsey had the governor playing with fire more than once. She, like many other chief executives, tried to reorganize the Department of Social and Health Services. DSHS is the state's largest department and consumes much of the state's budget. Governor Ray appointed a blue ribbon committee—in this case citizens from private industry—to help her with the reorganization. This committee, headed by Jerry Thompson, was successful in recommending the decentralization of "institutions," which eventually led to prisons and corrections becoming a separate department.

Scales of Justice

March 2, 1979

Brian Basset

Seattle Times

Here's Your Half!

Circa 1979

Alan Pratt

Seattle Times

Probably few court cases in Washington's first one hundred years have inflamed as much passion as the "Boldt Decision." The case began when the State of Washington became concerned that both white and native American fisherman were depleting a treasured natural resource— salmon. Many more whites than native Americans had come to depend on salmon for their livelihood, and white fishermen were catching 90 percent of the yearly run. The state secured a court order preventing the Puyallup Indian tribe from fishing in an area the state felt could destroy spawning grounds. The Puyallups, and eventually twenty-six other tribes, sued to protect treaty rights they felt were being violated.

On February 12, 1974 federal judge George Boldt heard arguments in Tacoma involving fishing rights granted from native Americans to non-native Americans by the Medicine Creek Treaty of 1854. In his decision Judge Boldt reaffirmed that under the United States Constitution treaties are the "supreme law of the land." He also agreed with the State of Washington that it had the power to regulate off-reservation Indian fishing, but only when it was necessary for the conservation of the salmon and when that regulation did not discriminate against treaty Indians.

The treaty said that native Americans have "the right of taking fish *in common* with all citizens of the territory." Judge Boldt decided that "in common" meant Indians were guaranteed 50 percent of the salmon caught off-reservations. The state appealed the decision first to the U.S. Circuit Court of Appeals, where the judges unanimously upheld Judge Boldt, and then to the Supreme Court of the United States. On July 2, 1979 the Supreme Court upheld Judge Boldt six to three. The cartoons of Alan Pratt and Brian Basset reflected much of the public's attitude about the decision.

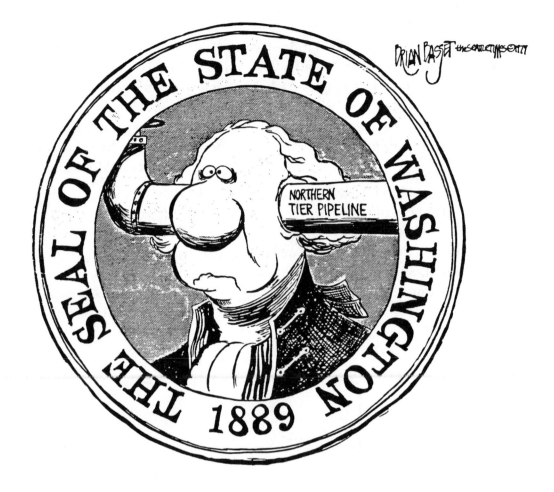

Northern Tier Pipeline Controversy

August 28, 1979

Brian Basset

Seattle Times

Washington was submerged in the Northern Tier controversy from the late 1970s to April 1982. Northern Tier wanted to build an oil terminal at Port Angeles and run a pipeline under Puget Sound across Admiralty Inlet, and then across the state and beyond to Minnesota. The federal government could have moved the nation's capital to our state during these years because so many officials were stopping in to "say hello" to Gov. John Spellman.

State law set up the Energy Facility Site Evaluation Council to review all energy projects affecting Washington. The law also made the governor the final decision maker for all energy applications. Even though Northern Tier and federal government officials were claiming that the pipeline was needed for national security reasons, the council concluded that Northern Tier's proposal was deficient in promises to protect the state's waters from oil spills and Port Angeles from possible tanker blasts. The council voted against the project. Through all of the attempted pressure, Governor Spellman remained firm in his support of the council decision.

1980–1989

Public Health Hospitals' Life Support

February 15, 1981

Brian Basset

Seattle Times

When the Reagan administration slated the closure of Public Health Service hospitals throughout the country in 1981, a massive community effort was mounted to save the PHS hospital in Seattle. Politicians, concerned citizens, and members of the medical community spearheaded the effort which resulted in the transfer of the hospital to a city-chartered public development authority known today as "Pacific Medical Center."

Since that time Pacific Medical Center has discontinued its inpatient operations to become one of the fastest growing providers of outpatient care in the Seattle area, with five satellite clinics throughout King County. Quality medical care is provided by members of a nonprofit provider group practice which includes about ninety physicians, dentists, optometrists, and other health professionals.

"HEY, CRASSUS! WE'VE BEEN CHOSEN AS THE EMPIRE'S MOST LIVEABLE CITY!"

The Most Livable City

April 13, 1980
David Horsey
Seattle Post-Intelligencer

David Horsey imagined a historical parallel as he and millions of other Washingtonians waited for Mt. Saint Helens to blow. Seattle had been chosen as the nation's most livable city not long before the volcano awoke on March 27, 1980.

Afterwards Saint Helens stayed relatively calm—like Vesuvius in Horsey's cartoon. But on the morning of May 18, 1980 people as far as two hundred miles away were jolted by a force equal to ten megatons of TNT. Centuries of forest growth were blasted away, the Toutle River became a flowing hell, and ash from the eruption began to circle the globe.

Tacoma Dome Controversy

Circa 1982

Myron Thompson

Tacoma News Tribune

A major issue that stirred up Pierce County and Tacoma in the early 1980s was the building of the Tacoma Dome. Nearly every resident had an opinion about how the dome should be built.

This Thompson cartoon shows the different factions that joined the fray. A Tacoma Dome "jury" of citizens was finally chosen to decide on design plans, and the Dome opened its doors to the public on April 21, 1983, on schedule and under budget. It is the largest wood domed structure in the world, and besides being a great facility for athletics, it is nationally known for its high concert-quality acoustics.

The Amazing Waffleman

Circa 1981
David Horsey
Seattle Post-Intelligencer

The 1980 gubernatorial race pitted John Spellman against Jim McDermott. Borrowing a technique from the cartoonists themselves—using a visual symbol to drive home a point—Spellman, during a debate, produced a breakfast waffle from his pocket. He waved the waffle through the air while accusing his opponent of "waffling" on the issues. The stunt backfired, however. Spellman was elected, but once in office he was accused of being indecisive and David Horsey pictured *him*, instead of his one-time opponent, as The Amazing Waffleman.

The Dependable Ferry System

January 29, 1982

Mike Luckovich

The University of Washington Daily

In 1951 Washington state took over the ferry system, and today its twenty-five ship ferry fleet can boast of being the largest and safest in the nation. But even our ferry system has had its mishaps, and it has become one of the most cartooned organizations in the state.

During the 1980s the state had multimillion dollar troubles with Marine Power and Equipment Company, the builder of the Issaquah-class ferries. Problems plagued the ferries' computer-controlled propulsion systems and contract disputes dragged on for years.

San Juan Islands residents also claimed that ferry captains tooted their horns in a courting ritual to local women. In October 1983 the ferry Elwha became folk history when it crashed into a reef off Orcas Island while its captain, Bill Fittro, was giving a passenger a private view of her island home from the bridge. Finally, during a two week period in September 1986, the ferry Cathlamet's brakes failed three times, once crashing into the Clinton dock on Whidbey Island.

The Titanic II

July 27, 1983
Shaw McCutcheon
Spokesman-Review

The Washington Public Power Supply System (WPPSS—pronounced Whoops) was created in 1957 by seventeen separate public utility districts. Its purpose was to build power plants and dams that many areas would need but that no district alone could afford. At first WPPSS provided hydroelectric power to its customers, but in 1968, anticipating a need for more power, WPPSS decided to go nuclear. The estimated cost of five plants at Satsop and Hanford skyrocketed from under $6 billion when the project began to $24 billion, making it the most expensive construction project in United States history.

After the leak at Three Mile Island, public opinion turned against the power plants, and only one plant has begun service.

The WPPSS story is far from over. In this cartoon, Shaw McCutcheon evokes the largest municipal-bond default in American history—$2 billion worth.

Monument to a Washington Monument

September 4, 1983

Brian Basset

Seattle Times

Henry M. Jackson was born in Everett in 1912. He was elected to the United States Senate six times and all but the first time by a margin of more than 65 percent. "Scoop" Jackson was called the "senator from Boeing" for his work on behalf of constituents, but he was widely honored as an honest and brilliant senator on all fronts.

Jackson rose to prominence as a critic of Sen. Joseph McCarthy during the Army hearings in 1954. He was regarded as a fiscal and defense-issue conservative but a social-policy liberal. During his tenure in the Senate he authored the Alaska and Hawaii statehood acts, the National Environmental Policy Act of 1970, and the 1980 Alaska Lands Act. Henry Jackson has been honored by having a mountain area named after him, and he was honored in this cartoon by Brian Basset.

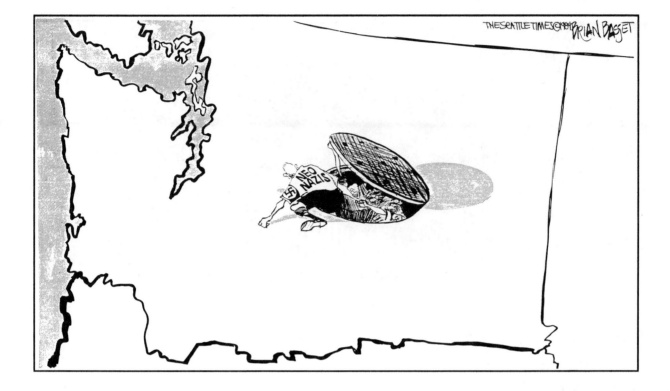

Sewer Dweller

December 19, 1984
Brian Basset
Seattle Times

Since the early 1980s when Richard Butler moved into North Idaho and founded the Aryan Nations, cartoonists have caricaturized neo-Nazis living in Washington. During the decade many neo-Nazis were linked to violent crime, and their movement was the target of a massive law-enforcement effort. One leader of the secret band known as The Order perished in a fiery shoot-out with the FBI at a house on Whidbey Island. Other neo-Nazis have been sent to prison for murder, racketeering, robbery, and illegal weapons possession.

Sir Winston Gardner

Circa 1986

Brian Basset

Seattle Times

The atomic reservation at Hanford has been the site of one of Washington's great debates. The focus of the debate is whether the federal government is dumping hazardous waste safely and whether Hanford should be the dumping ground for other states.

One of Brian Basset's favorite cartoons is this one of "Sir Winston Gardner." In October 1986 Gov. Booth Gardner led a crowd of one thousand people who linked hands across the Columbia River to protest the federal government's nuclear waste study at Hanford.

Most recently the U.S. Department of Energy stopped plutonium production at Hanford and put the nuclear reactor on "cold standby" because of a plutonium surplus. DOE's agreement to clean up the radioactive and toxic waste by 1995 could cost as much as $52 billion.

Home Sweet Home

June 3, 1987
Frank Shiers, Jr.
Port Orchard Independence

In 1984 the Vatican began a two-year investigation of Archbishop Raymond Hunthausen of Seattle and his ministry. Finding that Hunthausen had been lax in enforcing orthodox church teaching, the Vatican in January 1986 made Hunthausen surrender a significant portion of his authority to Auxiliary Bishop Donald Wuerl. Archbishop Hunthausen had generated national controversy because of his activism against nuclear weapons and his refusal to pay income taxes, but the Vatican stated that these were not factors in its disciplinary measures against Hunthausen.

People statewide and nationally were incensed that Hunthausen was deprived of responsibility in the areas of liturgical worship and statements concerning moral issues. In May 1987 Pope John Paul II restored Hunthausen's authority, but a coadjutor, Bishop Thomas J. Murphy, was named to assist the archbishop. The Pope is smiling in Shier's cartoon because a coadjutor has the right of succession.

Which Bank Will Be Next

March 4, 1987

Frank Shiers, Jr.

Tacoma News-Tribune

It is not too often that great white sharks enter the coastal waters of Washington, but when they do, they go after big prey. In August 1982 Rainier Bancorporation fell victim to the jaws of Security Pacific Bank of California. This attack left Puget Sound Bank as the last of the major independent public banks in Washington.

The devouring of independent banks in the 1980s has been bloody: Seafirst was swallowed up by California's Bank of America in July 1983, Old National Bank by U.S. Bank of Oregon in May 1987, Seattle Trust by Key Corp of New York in July 1987, and Peoples by U.S. Bank in December 1987. The only other major independent bank in the state is Washington Trust of Spokane, and it is privately owned.

Booth As A Gardner

February 21, 1988
Milt Priggee
Spokesman-Review

Washington state has seen many changes in its first one hundred years, but there is one thing that has not changed—the rivalry between the East and West sides. From the ferry system to school construction to road improvements to faculty salaries, East siders feel the West side growth is funded with East side dollars. In this cartoon, Milt Priggee comments on the perceived lip service that Governor Gardner gives to Spokane and the Inland Empire.

East County Comix

April 20, 1988

Steve Willis

East County News

Editorial cartoons are not limited to the major dailies. Steve Willis draws for a weekly in Grays Harbor County called the *East County News* which has a circulation of about ten thousand. His cartoons poke fun at the county's own residents and their political affiliations. In this cartoon Willis makes reference to the fact that Republicans are not very popular in Grays Harbor County. In fact they seldom appear on the county ballot. The county has voted Democratic in every presidential election since 1928. Yes, even McGovern and Mondale won.

Branches of Government

April 3, 1989
Steve Greenberg
Seattle Post-Intelligencer

The centennial legislature has been frequently cartooned. Steve Greenberg could not resist taking a swing at the Boeing Company for its resistance to tax reform. During the session Boeing tax director Joe Otani told the House Revenue Committee that he did not like the income tax plan. In a subsequent Seattle *Weekly* article Rebecca Boren reported that the Governor was "torqued" because Gardner had helped Boeing pass antitakeover legislation in 1987.

The question raised by Greenberg's cartoon is to what extent *does* Boeing control state lawmaking? The company employs one of every twenty Washingtonians, including a number of state legislators. When it comes time to voting or "vetoing," those figures have clout.

What About A Direct Primary

July 17, 1988

John Lavin

The Olympian

The old party pros of both the state Democratic and Republican parties have resisted for decades the direct presidential primary. In this cartoon John Lavin shows how the Democrats and Republicans have had to do quite a balancing act to keep away from this primary system. The parties have argued that the caucus system is better because it allows the voters an actual voice at neighborhood meetings and it permits the voters to become educated on the issues without being swayed by media blitzes.

Supporters of the presidential primary, on the other hand, have argued that party bosses are afraid of the primary because it would take control out of the bosses' hands and allow full participation by the general public. In March 1989 both houses of the state legislature passed Initiative 99, putting Washington among the majority of states holding direct presidential primaries.

Fun Things You Can Do With The State Minimum Wage

April 25, 1988

Steve Greenberg

Seattle Post-Intelligencer

The minimum wage in the State of Washington, one of the lowest in the country, had been raised only once since it was first enacted in 1959. As Steve Greenberg of the *Post-Intelligencer* pointed out, there is not much you can buy for $2.30 an hour. The public demanded an increase and, when the bill died in committee in 1988, took matters into its own hands and requested an initiative to raise the minimum wage to $3.85 an hour. Initiative 518 passed by a large margin.

SPOTTED OWL HABITATS OF:

MOTHER NATURE · U.S. FOREST SERVICE · TIMBER INDUSTRY

Spotted Owl Habitats

February 26, 1989

Milt Priggee

Spokesman-Review

The forests of Washington state have become a political combat zone between timber interests and environmentalists as a result of the northern spotted owl. Environmental groups have argued that the spotted owl is an endangered species and needs old-growth forests in order to survive. The U.S. Forest Service believes that timber sales do not threaten the spotted owl, and that setting aside 374,000 acres will assure its survival.

In 1989 the U.S. Fish and Wildlife Service temporarily listed the spotted owl as a threatened species, making large old-growth timber sales more difficult. However, since more mill town people vote than owls, this issue is far from being resolved.

Statehood Reenacted

November 1988

Robert Kelton

Citizen Observer

Spirit of 1989

November 11, 1988

Milt Priggee

Spokesman-Review

One of the favorite gags of cartoonists is to update historical events with modern characters and inventions. In these cartoons which celebrate the centennial, cartoonists Kelton and Priggee exaggerated two historical events to welcome Washington's statehood. Although Governor Ferry did receive a collect telegram from Benjamin Harrison, President Reagan, despite being conservative with the public dollar, did not charge the reenactment to Governor Gardner.

SPIRIT of 1989

Milt Priggee drew one of the most recognizable events in American history, the Spirit of '76, which celebrates America's independence. He substituted those characters with Washington's current leaders and suggested that a cartoonist's tools are just as much a part of this celebration. Tom Foley, Speaker of the U.S. House of Representatives, led the troops that include Gov. Booth Gardner and U.S. Sen. Slade Gorton, who had just completed a grueling election campaign.

Selected Washington Cartoonist Biographies

Sam Armstrong

Born in 1893, he joined the *Tacoma News Tribune* in 1918 as art editor. He drew editorial cartoons there for the next ten years and played a significant role in the development of art in the Northwest when he founded the Armstrong School of Art in Tacoma in 1923. Armstrong left Tacoma in 1929 for Santa Barbara, California where he became a member of an artist colony and made a reputation for himself as a mural decorator and portrait painter.

Brian Basset

Born in Connecticut in 1957, he began his cartooning career as a staff cartoonist for the *Ohio State Lantern* from 1975–78. He was selected as staff artist and editorial cartoonist for the *Detroit Free Press* during the summers of 1977 and 1978. Basset is currently editorial cartoonist for the *Seattle Times* and the creator of *Adam*, a syndicated comic strip with the Universal Press Syndicate.

Irwin Caplan

Born in 1919 in Seattle, Washington, he graduated from the University of Washington with a degree in fine arts. While in college he was staff cartoonist for the *Seattle Star*. After graduating from college, he became a freelance cartoonist, illustrator and graphic designer. Caplan was nominated for a Reuben three times and won the award in 1973 and again in 1982 as the top national advertising cartoonist for those years.

Ray Collins

Born on St. Patrick's Day in 1931, he joined the art department of the *Seattle Post-Intelligencer* in 1950. He created "Cecil C. Addle and Dipstick Duck," an editorial page comic strip that ran in the *P-I* from 1975–79. Collins signed on with the QUBE cable TV network (Columbus, Ohio) and worked as a video cartoonist until he became disabled by multiple sclerosis. He retired in 1984.

Walt Crowley

Born in 1947, he moved to Seattle in 1961. An avid cartoonist since childhood, he won several regional and national student art awards including honors for "Best Cartoon" in the *University of Washington Daily* in 1966. After a stint as an illustrator for Boeing, Crowley in 1967 joined the staff of *Helix*, Seattle's first underground newspaper, and contributed cartoons, cover illustrations, posters, editorial art, and writing until the paper's demise in 1970. Crowley then entered government and later formed a design agency with his wife Marie McCaffrey. He has retired his rapidograph and now works as a free-lance writer and consultant when not appearing as news commentator on Seattle's KIRO-TV.

Paul Fung

Born in 1897 in Seattle to Chinese Christian missionaries, he graduated from Franklin High School and began his career with the *Seattle Post-Intellingencer* art department in 1915. He left Seattle for New York in 1923 to work as comic strip assistant for Billy De Beck, creator of "Barney Google." Fung collaborated on such cartoon strips as "Gus and Gussie," "Bughouse Fables," and "Dumb Dora." He died in 1944.

Steve Greenberg

Born in 1954, he worked as an editorial cartoonist for the Los Angeles *Daily News* from 1978–84. He became editorial cartoonist for the *Seattle Post-Intelligencer* in 1985. His cartoons have won awards in regional, national, and international competitions every year since 1976. Most recently Greenberg has won awards from the Washington Press Association in 1988 and 1989.

Sam Groff

Born in 1902, he went to work for the *Seattle Star* as a combination artist and police reporter. He joined the *Seattle Times* in 1935 after his *Star* caricatures of General C. B. Blethan, the *Times* publisher, won Blethen's admiration. He reached the height of his popularity as a cartoonist with his pen-and-ink portrayals of the fortunes and vicissitudes of Seattle's Pacific Coast League baseball team in its quest for league titles. Groff died in 1950.

George Hager

Born in 1886, he was the son of former *Seattle Times* cartoonist John (Dok) Hager. A graduate of the University of Washington, he was a cartoonist for Seattle newspapers for seven years. After his father died in 1932, Hager carried on his father's cartoon featuring Dippy Duck for fifteen years in the *Christian Science Monitor*. He died in 1945.

John (Dok) Hager

Born in 1858, he came to Seattle in 1899 to practice dentistry. His interest in caricature prompted him to join the *Seattle Times* staff in the early years of the twentieth century. He was the creator of Dok's "Dippy Duck" cartoons that ran in the *Times* for nineteen years. His familiar cartoon portraying his duck and the umbrella man appeared daily with the weather notices in the *Times* until failing eyesight forced him to retire. He died in 1932.

David Horsey

Born in 1950, he began his career in journalism as a political reporter and cartoonist for the Bellevue *Daily Journal-American* from 1976–79, after graduating from the University of Washington with a degree in journalism. He also earned an M.A. in international relations as a Rotary Foundation scholar at the University of Kent in England in 1986. He has won six first place awards for editorial cartooning in Northwest regional competitions. Horsey is the creator of the nationally syndicated cartoon strip "Boomers Song."

Robert Kelton

Born in 1955, he first considered a career in art after the Air Force asked him to do posters and cartoons for base activities. He graduated from the Art Institute of Seattle in 1987 and currently works as a pasteup artist while free-lancing as an illustrator and cartoonist. In 1987 Kelton won first and second places in the Sigma Delta Chi Excellence in Journalism competition for cartooning and illustrating for non-daily publications in western Washington.

John Lavin

Born in 1964, he received a B.A. in art from Western Washington University in 1986. He worked as a summer intern in 1984 as staff artist for *The Olympian*, and drew two cartoons a week for *Western Front*, Western Washington University's student newspaper. Lavin received the Society of Professional Journalists "Mark of Excellence" award for editorial cartooning in regional competition in 1985 and 1986, and its national award in 1985. He is now in his fifth year as cartoonist for *The Olympian*.

Mike Lukovich

Born in 1960, he attended the University of Washington from 1978–82. He cartooned for *The University of Washington Daily* and graduated with a degree in political science. For two years he sold life insurance before receiving his first editorial cartooning job with the *Greenville News* in South Carolina. In 1985 Lukovich joined the *New Orleans Times Picayune* and was a Pulitzer Prize finalist in 1986. In May 1989 he joined the *Atlanta Staff Constitution*.

Fred Marshall

Born in 1904, he came to the *Seattle Post-Intelligencer* in 1934 as head artist and cartoonist in the promotion department. He worked for the *P-I* for thirty-seven years and contributed drawings to the editorial page of the *P-I* under the banner "Twas Ever Thus on Puget Sound" from 1961–71. Marshall, a distinguished watercolor painter, was one of the few Northwest painters selected for membership by the American Watercolor Society. He died in 1979.

Bob McCausland

Born in 1915, he studied art at Edison Vocational School before joining the *Seattle Post-Intelligencer* editorial art staff in 1945. He was known for his creation of the "Hairbreadth Husky" in 1959 which told the good and bad fortunes of the University of Washington Husky football team. McCausland retired in 1979, but he keeps busy drawing a weekly cartoon for the *Aberdeen Daily World* and doing wood carvings.

Shaw McCutcheon

Born in 1921 into a newspaper family, he graduated from Harvard University in 1943 in mathematics. He began doing editorial cartoons for the Spokane *Spokesman-Review* in 1950 and remained there for the next thirty-six years. He retired in 1986. He currently spends much of his time in Spokane playing golf and achieving what many golfers only hope to do—shooting their age.

William C. Morris

Born in 1874, he worked for the Spokane *Spokesman-Review* from 1904–13, and from there rose to international prominence in the field of editorial cartooning. He also served as cartoonist for the *New York Tribune*, the *New York Mail*, the George Mathew Adams Syndicate, *Harpers Weekly*, and other publications. In the 1936 presidential campaign Morris drew cartoons for the National Republican Committee. He died in 1940.

Jim North

Born in 1878, he came to Tacoma around the turn of the century from Washington, D.C. and worked for the *Tacoma News* for fifteen years during which time his cartoons were potent factors in national, state, and local politics. Later he joined the *Washington Post* as its political cartoonist. North's cartoons were frequently reproduced in magazines such as the *Literary Digest*, *Time*, and *Newsweek*. He died in 1944.

Walt Partymiller

Born in Seattle in 1911, he graduated from Roosevelt High School in 1930. His first cartoons were printed in the University of Washington *Columns*, where he drew cover drawings. He worked on the staff of the *Seattle Post-Intelligencer* from 1933–36, then attended art school in New York. He was chief cartoonist for the *New Dealer* and the *New World*, radical papers in Washington state, and even after he moved back East he continued to appear in Washington state papers via syndication. Partymiller became the cartoonist of the York (Pa.) *Gazette and Daily* in 1945 and was notable for being the cartoonist in the only daily in America to support Henry Wallace for President in 1948. Now retired, Walt is married to the granddaughter of F. Opper, one of the founding fathers of the American comic strip.

Alan Pratt

Born in 1922 into a newspaper family, he joined the *Seattle Times* in 1942. He remained with the *Times* forty-one years as staff artist, news art director and chief artist until his retirement in 1983. Pratt currently writes and illustrates fishing articles and books from his woodsy homestead near Woodinville when these activities do not interfere with his fishing.

G. Stuart Pratt

Born in 1895, he came to Seattle in 1919 where he worked as a news artist at the *Seattle Post-Intelligencer* for ten years. He joined the *Seattle Times* staff in 1929 and became chief artist and director of the department eight years later. Pratt retired in 1965 and died in 1977.

Milt Priggee

Born in 1953, he graduated from Adams State College in Alamosa, Colorado in 1976 with a major in fine arts. After college he met his mentor, John Fischetti, who helped him start freelancing his cartoons for the Chicago *Tribune*, *Sun-Times* and *Daily News*. He became a regular cartoonist for the weekly *Crain's Chicago Business*, and then worked for the Dayton, Ohio *Journal-Herald* from 1982–86. Priggee began working for the Spokane *Spokesman-Review* and *Chronicle* in 1987 where he draws seven cartoons a week on local, national and world topics. He is the winner of Mencken Awards from the Associated Press Society of Ohio and of contests sponsored by the National Newspaper Association, the Overseas Press Club, and the Small Business Foundation of America.

Frank Shiers

Born in Bremerton in 1955, he graduated from Washington State University in 1977. He first drew his "T. R." comic strip for the college newspaper, and began political cartooning in 1979. He is syndicated to thirteen different newspapers throughout Western Washington, where his cartoons are seen by more people then any other cartoonist in the state. Shiers has won fourteen state and regional awards and is the recipient of the Best Political Cartooning award from the National Newspaper Association.

Myron Thompson

Born in 1938, he worked for the *Seattle Times* as staff artist from 1967–70. He joined the *Tacoma News Tribune* in 1970 and became art director in 1973. Thompson created two cartoons, "Big Olaf" and "Bumper," which ran in the Sunday *News Tribune* from 1974–82 and 1978–81 respectively.

Tom Thurlby

Born in England in 1876 with a crippled shoulder, he came to America when he was a young boy. He began his career with the *Minneapolis Tribune* and came to Seattle around 1905, joining the *Seattle Post-Intelligencer* as cartoonist. In 1915 he went to the *Seattle Times* where he remained until his death in 1928.

Steve Willis

Born in Washington, he attended Evergreen State College where he worked on the *Cooper Point Journal* alongside Matt Groening, Lynda Barry, and Charlie Burns. He established an academic collection of comics at Washington State University while working there as a librarian. Willis currently draws "East County Comix" for *East County News Weekly*.